RECAPTURING AMERICA

By Joseph Ehrlich

Notice to Readers of Recapturing America

Recapturing America employs ***fictional conversational techniques*** with political and public figures to raise and address public issues and concerns. Those issues include but are not limited to electing public officials a) who will serve without conflict of interest; b) warranting the public trust; and c) who will investigate whether government is carrying out covert agendas not in accord with the best interests of the Nation. *Recapturing America* defines the best interests of the Nation as assuring a government which tells the American people the truth, rather than a government which keeps hidden agendas, or a government which otherwise lies to and deceives the public, including doing so, under a guise and facade of national interests and/or national security. *A government in true service of its citizens acts to assure the American public true choice in the election process, by opposing any actions by anyone, including outside special interest groups, to limit true, free choice and/or candidates out of step with existing governmental policies or agendas.* A government serving the best interests of the Nation is further defined as one which warrants that it will not impinge upon the responsibilities of the public media to expose or speak against government policies and agendas, *nor one which covertly exercises, by actions otherwise seemingly legal, any indirect or direct influence or control over the media, including any actions discouraging, in any means or fashion, aggressive investigation, discussion and criticism of government policies and agendas.* In this manner, *Recapturing America*, while a novel and work of fiction, aims to serve the public interest and good. ***All conversations and events should be deemed completely fictional, at minimum, and, at best, matters of artistic expression and opinion.***

ISBN: 978-0-6151-4037-7

Library of Congress Control Number: 2007900750

First Print Edition, January 2007

Published by Sender, Berl & Sons Inc. / New York. Incorporated 1978.

(212) 927-7582.

Also by the author: Clarity By Joseph Ehrlich (ISBN: 978-0-6151-4142-8)

Dedicated to my children, Markus and Lysha.

Contents

Chapter 1
The Presidential Motorcade

When my landlady ultimately sold her townhouse at 27th and P Street in Georgetown, Washington D.C. in 1974 for $95,000, I thought she made out like a bandit. Years later, however, that same townhouse sold upwards of $500,000. Georgetown was the place for many Washington insiders to live, as I should have realized years before, when I waved many nights at Richard Nixon, as he traveled up P street, at 11:00 PM, for meetings with neighbor Averell Harriman.

To explain why Richard Nixon, one night, not only stopped, but sat with me on the stoop of the townhouse, I have to relay the first time we met.

I was a student at George Washington University Law School, blocks from the White House, but for a change in environment, I often went to the American University Library to study at night.

I knew the back roads of Washington well, and I was using Cleveland Avenue to get to Calvert to cut into Rock Creek Parkway, which would take me back to the townhouse, after a night's study at AU. However, this one night, there were a lot of lights and activity on Calvert. I instantly knew that the President was at the Shoreham Hotel.

You first must understand that security was much less intense in the late 60s than today. You could literally walk into any government building and go where you please. My own favorite place to do special study projects was the library at the U.S. Supreme Court. This great library was usually totally vacant except for a number of librarians there to serve any attorney using it (which usually meant attorneys present in Washington preparing to argue before the Supreme Court of the United States).

Nevertheless, while other students at law school were moving through the stacks to get their federal and state reporter case books, I had several librarians at the Supreme Court more than happy to do all the retrievals for me. It gave them something to do, and I always questioned why no one else, in all my three years in Washington, ever discovered this best kept secret.

In the late 60s, Washington was a warm, friendly and open town. If you walked down the streets where embassies were located, you could walk in and join a party and partake in Washington's favorite activity: drinking booze.

So that night, I simply pulled my car over and double parked on the south side of Calvert, stepped out, and leaned against the car expecting the President to come out of the Shoreham Annex, since, in front of it, were some fifty plus reporters and cameramen ready for action.

And some three or four minutes later, he stepped out. I was surprised at the depth of the rouge about his face, and he seemed jovial, waving, and atypical for me, when I thought he was looking at me, I said "Good evening, Mr. President." Now, I didn't know then if he recognized me from the doorsteps of the townhouse, but, to my total surprise, he walked around the Presidential limousine, came right up to me, and shook my hand focusing it seems only on me, with a warm and gracious smile.

Immediately, the open Secret Service limousine backed up right to the President, and an agent, in what I thought was a very gruff manner, directed the President to his limousine by shouting: "Mr. President, get into the car." He obliged the command.

I also got a command from the same agent: "You! Get into your car." I did. And the most unbelievable set of quick events occurred. The open Secret Service limousine directed the Presidential limousine to move ahead of it, behind two closed secret service cars, and the police standing right there directed me to follow the open Secret Service car. The next thing I knew I was part of the Presidential motorcade moving onto Rock Creek Parkway.

The parkway was closed to traffic due to the Presidential motorcade heading back to the White House. The motorcade consisted of the following: two cars in front of the Presidential limousine, the open Secret Service car, me, and two cars behind me; the car directly behind me, a station wagon with a single driver.

The secret service agents really look all over the place. To the best of my recollection, there were, at least, six of them in the back of the open secret service limousine, looking up, looking down, looking right, looking left all the time. And there was me, with my driver's side window open, my left elbow resting on the door, and my heart racing, saying: "This is really unbelievable."

I was staring at the secret service agents because while they were looking every which way, no one at first seemed to be looking straight back. Then finally one did, and I could read his lips without any experience in lip reading. His lips moved and I had no doubt what he was saying to his fellow agents: "Who the hell is that?"

One of the agents picked up a phone, and then the two cars in front of the President's, and the Presidential limousine, took off, like the wind, with the Secret Service car laying behind manifestly to block me from trying to follow and permitting the President's "safe escape."

At the very same moment, the station wagon behind me went to my right and tried to force me over to the side of the road. It was right then I made, what today, would certainly be, a fatal error.

Since I had no electric windows, I stretched down across the car to manually open the passenger side window. For several moments, I was out of site. It was a stupid mistake but once I got the window basically open, I started yelling, "What are you trying to do!"

The open Secret Service limousine then accelerated out of site, as we were approaching the end of Rock Creek Parkway at the Watergate Apartment site. There, I saw I had earned a large reception committee, with at least a dozen government and D.C. police cars waiting for me.

One agent held up his hand directing me to stop. To offset the stupidity of my disappearing act when I opened the passenger window, I pulled out my George Washington University Law School ID. Before the Secret Service or FBI agent (I was too nervous then to now recall which) could open his mouth, as he approached me with his entourage of law enforcement officials, I said: "It's not my fault. You guys directed me behind the Secret Service car. The President came up to me, shook my hand. Then they told him to get into his car and me to get into my car and to follow the Secret Service car. I'm a law student at George Washington University. Here's my ID."

Before he would look at my ID, he started reciting one of the numerous unknown laws where you can get arrested for anything the government wants. This one was that it was a crime to travel within 500 feet of a Presidential motorcade. Of course, my point was that there was no crime when I am directed by the government and police to be part of it.

They looked at the ID; spoke for less than sixty seconds, and told me I could go.

My heart was racing. I was excited. I wanted to catch up to the motorcade all over again, but reason prevailed. When it did, I found myself only a couple of blocks from the GW Law School Library. I went over there to share the story with some of my friends and classmates.

CHAPTER 2
THE DOORSTEP

So, when months later, President Nixon's limousine did stop in front of the townhouse at 27th and P, when he saw me, I finally found out that he did recognize me from his constant travels to neighbor Averell Harriman, who the President considered one of the most astute minds in the country.

I told him about the motorcade incident and he laughed. He actually sat down on the doorstep and I immediately invited him in and he accepted.

When he went to Averell Harriman's house, he traveled with one driver and another car with two secret service agents. In today's highly protective environment for Presidents, it may be difficult for some to imagine how relatively informal Washington was in those days; not to belittle having the President of the United States come into the townhouse for a chat.

To Richard Nixon, it was probably going to be a relatively quick hello, what are you studying, where are you from, and come over for a specially arranged tour of the White House. However, for me, his visit to my home was a window of opportunity, where I had access to one of the most powerful men in the world. I wasn't at all as interested in his power, as touching him for his knowledge.

What I was especially interested in was the assassination of John F. Kennedy, the lone gunman theory, and the complacency of the public and the government to seek or speak the truth.

One of the other tenants in the townhouse, who became a good friend of mine during our time in Washington, was from a family who were very big contributors to the Republican Party. I immediately told the President that their son lived in my townhouse and that really made the President smile. So it made it much easier for me to give the President the opening line in what I was interested in pursuing with him.

"I just don't understand why Kennedy is going down in the history books as such a great President, when we all know he was one of the worst. If they name one more Boulevard for him, I think I am going to get sick."

"Well, Noah," the President commenced in response, "when you are President of the United States and you get assassinated in office, the country is going to make you a heroic figure, whether you deserve it or not." I could see the President was thinking whether he should say anything more.

"But Mr. President, making someone a heroic figure who among other things was a womanizer even when President of the United States and had no respect for his wife, his children, not to say his country, I think is wrong."

The President looked directly at me. I think he was evaluating whether to say anything at all or to leave.

Then I quipped, "When Marilyn Monroe came out on national TV to sing Happy Birthday Mr. President, it was a disgrace, a near sexual act, which made me embarrassed to watch with my family in the same room."

That broke the ice.

"Well, Noah, he's no longer President. I am sure many Americans join you in your feelings about it. How old were you then, Noah, when you watched Marilyn Monroe sing at Madison Square Garden?"

"Fifteen I answered."

Richard Nixon then asked me the question I direly wanted him to ask.

"Do you think others than Oswald were involved in the assassination?"

I was then given the chance of impressing the President of the United States, not knowing how much risk I might have put myself under.

"Mr. President. In all honesty, I carefully watched the Kennedy videos and it seems clear to me that any intelligent person could only conclude one bullet struck President Kennedy from the back, which threw him forward, causing Mrs. Kennedy to respond, and then a second bullet struck him from his right side seconds later throwing his head backwards."

"My question, Noah, in our little chat which I take it will remain between us, is who do you think was behind Kennedy's assassination if not solely Oswald?"

I didn't then know why President Nixon was so interested in my opinion.

"My personal feeling is that President Johnson, J. Edgar Hoover and one other person were the central figures in the assassination."

"You're a law student at George Washington University, Noah. You are an intelligent young man and so I am interested in your thinking about the connection between Johnson and Hoover. I thought they didn't like one another?"

Before I relay what I said to the President, I want to emphasize to you, that my point and desire in this window of opportunity, was to enlist some hint on why the government was so disdainful in letting the public in on the truth.

I told the President first that I knew the little known fact that J. Edgar Hoover and President Johnson were once good neighbors, living, for many years, right across the street from one another. President Nixon was very impressed that I even knew where J. Edgar Hoover lived.

I also told the President that I knew that J. Edgar Hoover was gay, and that this fact presented a conflict of interest, when J. Edgar Hoover was the only person in America who denied the existence of organized crime.

Next, I told the President that I could see in Lyndon Johnson's face the torment and turmoil in standing subservient to a younger man; a younger man for whom he had no respect, as a person or as a President. Lyndon Johnson was a man who simply couldn't stomach his relationship with John F. Kennedy.

This synergy tied in with the open interest of organized crime in getting rid of Bobby Kennedy who had an overt fixation in ridding America and its labor unions of organized crime. Marilyn Monroe and other women were directed to Bobby Kennedy, so that organized crime could put pressure on Bobby Kennedy, as they had, with men, on J. Edgar Hoover.

When Bobby Kennedy told his brother about Marilyn Monroe, things looked even better for organized crime, when she went over to the President of the United States. However, organized crime couldn't get the Kennedys to react as they did J. Edgar Hoover. Instead of striking a deal, the Kennedys didn't respond well to attempted extortion: instead of bending in to organized crime, they turned up the heat on organized crime.

The link between organized crime and Lyndon Johnson was J. Edgar Hoover. Johnson was one of the most corrupt politicians in Washington, but distant from organized crime. The mutual umbrella of hatred for John F. Kennedy and his brother, Robert, brought three of the most powerful forces in America together: organized crime, J. Edgar Hoover and Lyndon Johnson.

"What about the third central figure? You didn't name him," the President interjected, looking at his watch, indicating that my time with him was running short.

I was embarrassed to tell him my thoughts about the third figure. However, he was asking me and I told him.

"Jackie Kennedy," I said.

I thought the President and the Secret Service agent in the room were going to leave. But the President said, "Go on."

"Mr. President, I believe Mrs. Kennedy with a single word could have uprooted the lone gunman theory and the Warren Commission report."

"So why didn't she?" the President inquired.

"That is what exactly got me asking some basic questions," Mr. President. "Why didn't she speak out?"

I continued: "After the incident with Marilyn Monroe, Mrs. Kennedy must have been furious. She knew her husband was less than loyal, but this incident with Marilyn Monroe was a public insult, a black eye, to her and their children. This is exactly when, Mr. President, strong rumors first surfaced about a possible divorce."

"Mr. President," I went on, "Marilyn Monroe sang Happy Birthday Mr. President and Thanks for the Memory to President Kennedy in May, 1962. However, by the time of the assassination, Mrs. Kennedy and the President were enjoying a rejuvenation in their relationship."

"So, Noah, doesn't that undermine what you are saying?" the President asked me.

"Well, Mr. President. . .if Kennedy wasn't assassinated in the midst of this renewal period in their relationship, then it obviously would have been a genuine attempt to put their relationship back together. However, when the fact is that the President gets assassinated, it makes someone like me suspicious."

"Suspicious about what?" the President echoed.

"Suspicious about whether Mrs. Kennedy's especially warm, openly warm, unusually warm behavior towards the President just prior to his assassination, wasn't a little obtuse considering their mutual threats of divorce and knowing her husband's propensity to cheat behind her back."

The President sat quietly waiting for me to continue.

"What did Mrs. Kennedy hold most dear to her, above everything else?" I asked the President.

"Her children."

"Correct," I replied.

"Her children were her world. She lived for them, Mr. President, " I said. "Now, Mr. President, if President Kennedy pursued a divorce, which I admit he was unlikely to, during his Presidency, but if he did, or if she pursued a divorce, as was more likely at the time, who would get custody of the children?"

"Yes, Noah, the President would have kept custody if that was his preference," President Nixon plainly stated.

"And if this divorce occurred after the President left office, President Nixon, what chances do you think Mrs. Kennedy thought she might have in securing custody at a later date or time?"

"Yes, Noah, she was no match for her husband."

"And Mr. President, after the Marilyn Monroe incident, Mrs. Kennedy wanted out. She didn't however know how. She was stuck, and everyone knew it including Johnson and Hoover, both of whom needed Mrs. Kennedy to bring their agendas to reality."

Lyndon Johnson who was a real Texan, bold and brazen, as he was immodest, had to somehow see if he could get Jackie Kennedy into the plot.

Lyndon Johnson knew that no matter how dedicated and loyal Mrs. Kennedy may be to her office of First Lady, this was a black eye for her and her children. The behind the back gossip she and her children were facing was insufferable. He also knew that she well knew that if she planned on one day divorcing the President, as no doubt she wanted to (and no doubt he wanted her to do too), that there would be no way she would ever get custody over her children – whom she lived for, loved and adored.

Thus, these various forces came to a head when Jackie Kennedy had to agree to participate in the assassination plot, because she otherwise could single handily blow to ribbons all other efforts to cover up the truth of what really happened that day. She knew the damage done to the President came from shots coming from two different directions; she knew the driver slowed to an unwarranted speed; she knew what was being said in the limousine; what really happened at the hospital; she knew what was being covered up; she knew that everything that would come from the Warren Commission was cover up, replete with lies. And if she, Jackie Kennedy, spoke up, just several words, *saying to the effect the Warren Report was an insult or lie to her and the Nation*, she could unravel any effort to suppress the truth. She had to be a player. *She had, in view of what she saw as an impending divorce, good reason to be.*

Johnson and Hoover, no doubt, considered shooting Jackie too. However, this posed serious concerns: killing both President and First Lady, by supposedly a single gunman; and leaving the children orphans. The country then for sure would not tolerate receiving anything less than convincing answers and justice.

Jackie Onasis' (Jackie O's) life and actions since the assassination were consistent with her being a player, happy to live a life as a totally private person and dedicated and loving mother and parent to her children.

The assassination took place in Dallas Texas, Johnson's home territory. All the activity, including necessary documentation, was under the control of Hoover, and then Johnson, as President of the United States; being sworn in, ironically due to proclaimed fears of a conspiracy, swiftly on Air Force One with Mrs. Kennedy at his side.

John F. Kennedy received the honors and funeral he didn't deserve, in the eyes of those who proffered to serve the Nation, by assuring his immediate exit from office. John F. Kennedy would no longer disgrace the Nation. His reward would be that history would honor him to further cover up the true dynamics that moved events and powerful people to cause his death.

President Nixon stood up to leave. He looked at me and said: "What a vivid imagination." He turned his back and left without saying another word. I thought I would never hear or see him again. I was sure that he would never stop by the house again. and I was right about that but I was wrong about not seeing him again.

CHAPTER 3
THE GUARD DOG

One of the best teacher's I ever had in Washington, D.C. was a guard dog whose name escapes me after all these years.

When I first started at law school, I lived in a first floor apartment on California Street. Stationed, literally outside my door, were a security guard and a guard dog.

On my return from class, I always encountered the same guard and guard dog.

The dog was a white German Shepherd. I loved animals, particularly German Shepherds. During my college years, I even trained the German Shepherd belonging to the family of a close friend.

After knowing this dog for seven months, petting it, feeding it, and knowing that he well knew me, one day, the dog gave me one of the most important lessons of my life.

I was talking with the guard about guard dog training and I asked whether he thought, if he commanded his dog to attack me, that he would. He didn't blink when he said that if he gave the dog the command, the dog would tear me to ribbons.

I couldn't accept that a dog that I knew liked me, who I petted and fed for so many months, could master the psyche to do what the guard told me he surely would do on the command to do so. I really didn't even think this dog could find it in himself to bark at me, yet say, growl at me.

The guard held the dog firmly by the leash and gave the dog a command and this dog, who knew me and liked me, went for me with a passion to kill me. His face, his attitude, his body, his entire psyche, in a moment's time, went from kind and loving to one which would kill me without apparent remorse or conscience.

So several years later, after I started working in New York for one of the country's leading attorney's, I remembered this dog and the lesson he taught me.

I had the privilege to work with the great Joseph E. Brill of New York. You probably never heard of him because he was a lawyer's lawyer and thus when the infamous Roy Cohen needed a lawyer, he turned to Joseph E. Brill.

Working and learning from such a master was a lifetime experience. It also gave me the opportunity to learn from some of the leading legal figures who ever lived, including Roy Cohen – who himself, when not a defendant, was the most feared attorney in New York and was counsel in the 50s to Senator Joe McCarthy and the McCarthy hearings; Harry S. Lipsig, the dean of personal negligence attorneys, and Milton Gould of Shea & Gould, the attorney the *New York Times* rated as the first, second and third most powerful attorney in New York.

After my first case working with Joe Brill, which we won, he and the clients sent me on what they thought was a well-earned week's vacation in Acapulco, Mexico. They got me a beautiful suite at the Hyatt Regency. This turned out to be much more of a vacation than I bargained for.

When I got off the plane and finished with customs, I was walking to pick up my luggage. Some 100 feet from me, I looked upon, what I thought then and now to be, the most beautiful, fashionably dressed, woman I ever saw in my life.

She was wearing a Faye Dunaway type broadband hat. She was tall, elegant and simply beautiful. I remember the very thought that crossed my mind when I saw her: lucky is the guy who is with her. She had come off a plane from Dallas, Texas, and she looked the fitting wife or girl friend of some big, rich Texas oil Baron.

Now while this story is going to sound like one which books are written about, it is genuinely true. I picked up my luggage, went into a cab, and told the driver to take me to the Hyatt Hotel. That beautiful woman already was out of my mind, as one of the fleeting events and thoughts of life itself.

I could not believe that when I entered the hotel to check in, she was at the registration desk! I couldn't believe she was staying there. It looked like she was by herself, and I couldn't understand how she got there before me, since it appeared she was waiting for her luggage at the Braniff baggage area, when I saw her at the airport.

My heart started racing. That's how beautiful she was and I was saying could fate really have put us so close.

She checked in and left for her room. However, still in an emotional cloud about her beauty, I next couldn't figure out my luck when I went to the elevator and she was in it when it opened. She wasn't getting out, and, while surprised, I wasn't thinking about anything but how pleased I was that she was remaining in the elevator. I went in, with the porter, to take my luggage to the room.

In the elevator, she smiled at me and I, who must have been beside myself with the way things were going, was truly bold enough to start a conversation with her.

In the span of seconds, she acknowledged she was there for a short stay and I, after I told her I was there by myself for a short vacation too, asked her if she had any dinner plans. She said no, and right there she agreed to have dinner with me that evening.

I'm not a bad looking fellow, but this was a goddess of a woman. I didn't belong with her as was evident when every man from customer to waiter to busboy to cab driver starred at her that evening and then looked at me and asked the question I was asking myself.

However, I really enjoyed dinner with her and we had a great time. We spoke about different things and I recognized that she had a good mind to go with that gorgeous figure. I told her that if the rest of my stay went like the dinner I was going to enjoy this trip to Mexico.

When we got back to the hotel from the restaurant, we went to sit on chaise lounges by the beach. A fellow doesn't know what to think, but I could see that she really seemed to enjoy being with me out there, and after a while, as a cool breeze came between us, she snuggled next to me.

It was either the natural beauty of Acapulco, the change of environment for both of us, or something beyond both of us, when next, in the most natural and beautiful manner, we started kissing. Deep long passionate kissing.

With the increase in the excitement in both our bodies, my hands moved towards her breasts. Perfect breasts. Large breasts with bursting nipples which reacted erotically with every stroke of my hands and the more passionate moves of our mouths and bodies.

It was so beautiful, natural and exciting, having consummate intimacy right out there on the beach in front of the hotel. When it was over, she wanted to stand up and seemed to reflect surprise at her own reactions and emotions. Her body trembled, as she took several steps, and she said she was going to her room.

I let her go, planning on knocking on her door in an hour. I sat there in one of the most beautiful places in the world reflecting on the pleasure and the conquest of a woman whom I saw as one of the most beautiful women in the world.

Afterwards, about one hour later, she wouldn't really let me in her room. She opened the door, and I could see she had first quality luggage on her bed with an array of outfits, which would indicate that she could dress for any occasion. She told me she would see me tomorrow.

And while she saw me and we had dinner two more times the remainder of the week, she was distant with me until the last day we would be in Acapulco together.

I didn't know what to really think but that she was asking herself what someone like her was doing with someone like me that first night. And she, in subsequent days, would sit at the outdoor bar with strapping sculptured muscle bound Roman warrior types of guys at her beck and call. However, I saw she never went off with any of them.

On the last day together, I figured it out for sure and admitted the truth. We spoke about her. I could see something was bothering her and she was sad. I simply started the conversation that last day by asking her why someone like herself, who was thirty-two, wasn't already settled down with someone and a family. She had told me she never married.

She now told me she had a boy friend, but one who didn't appreciate her. I couldn't understand that, I told her, because she was not only beautiful but I knew sensitive and intelligent. By the time she left the hotel, I knew she very much liked me as a person, and I couldn't feel anything but positively towards a person who gave me what I still consider a lifetime experience.

Of course, I also knew by then that she was sent there for me. No one has all this kind of luck. The way she positioned herself, no doubt, at the airport; being at the counter of the very hotel I was staying at; being in the elevator when I was first going to my room; giving me a warm and friendly look; being receptive to my invitation; being with me, not to say having sex with me, which I happily remember as one I believe she was surprised in enjoying herself, even though her wardrobe showed me she was a professional.

She was there to report on me. My sexual preferences; what I spoke about; what I thought about; what I cared about; how I carried myself; to provide a psychological profile for someone. Who?

The answer was not too long in coming. In June 1973, I received a call from the White House inviting me to a breakfast with the President of the United States. I then figured out that I got a good report and before seeing Richard Milhous Nixon again, I was thanking him sincerely, in my mind, for a very memorable vacation. I also knew that Christine, I very well remember her name, was like the guard dog on California Street. With the very same aplomb she carried out her assignment with me, she could one day have me in her room and put a knife in my back. Knowing that, was the only thing which spoiled making me love the woman. At least I could always love the memory.

CHAPTER 4
NIXON SHOULDN'T HAVE STOPPED AT 27TH & P.

When I was invited for breakfast, and greatly honored by the invitation, I did not expect to be sitting alone with the President. Thus, I knew that something special was up and it connected with my "vivid imagination" talk with the President, and the report from Christine.

In November 1972, Nixon and Agnew won re-election. Within months, an investigation commenced against Spiro Agnew, a sitting Vice-President of the United States.

Usually any criminal action against such a high official would be reluctantly pursued. This one was dominant in the news each day, and nearly immediately Agnew was subject to intense pressure to resign from office.

"Noah, I asked you to the White House, because I want to ask you a question."

"Mr. President, what can I say but that I am greatly honored, and I hope I can give you an answer which will prove helpful."

"Everyone here in the White House and in Washington have their own agendas. I get so many different types of opinions, that I really don't get any advice I feel I can rely on. I needed to hear something different and from someone different from the rest of the people I know here."

I guess I knew what the President was saying.

"Spiro Agnew will soon resign as Vice-President of the United States. You may have heard the rumors about my intent to appoint Nelson Rockefeller in his place. Using that vivid imagination of yours, would you tell me whether you think this could be an error on my part."

I knew exactly what the President was worried about, and I agreed with his concerns, and I simply told him so.

"Mr. President, Nelson Rockefeller has attempted to get the Republican Presidential nomination three times. All without success. The reasons are known: people in general are put off by the wealth, stealth, power and ambition of the Rockefeller family."

"The very fact that you called me to the White House to ask me this question shows me you have grave concerns about putting Nelson Rockefeller in as Vice-President. And since you called me, it is obvious that what you fear is that the Rockefellers may not wait until 1976 to get the Republican nomination. You are worried that they are thinking like Lyndon Johnson in 1963."

"Are my fears so apparent to you, Noah?"

I knew what the President wanted to hear.

"With good reason Mr. President. My father taught me that it is good policy not to pursue a course you carry concerns about, especially when you have numerous alternatives. By appointing Nelson Rockefeller, you are just going to give yourself headache and heartache for three years. It's not healthy or pleasant to always look behind your back." I was thinking about the guard dog, when I said that to him.

Contrary to his restraint at the townhouse, the President opened up to me.

"The problem is that I made a deal with the Rockefellers. After the Watergate break in, the situation was one that could have compromised the November elections... Nelson Rockefeller told me that the entire episode would be a non-event for the elections. He said he could control the media. He would appreciate it, however, if I could, after the elections, get rid of Agnew and appoint him Vice-President."

This time I sat there in silence hoping that he would say something more. Since I didn't, he did.

"But you're right. I'm never going to sleep if I appoint him Vice-President. He's too ambitious. He can't wait like Johnson and like Johnson he doesn't believe he will ever win unless he's in by default first."

I was getting nervous because Richard Nixon was saying a lot more than I should have ever heard.

He honored me further by asking: "How would you advise me if I wanted to break the deal? The Rockefellers will not be happy."

"Thanks for telling me that, Mr. President," I thought to myself.

"If you don't appoint Nelson Rockefeller, Mr. President whom will you appoint?"

"Gerald Ford."

"Does he want to run for President in 1976?"

"Who doesn't," President Nixon said sarcastically. "But Gerald Ford is a good man. He will cooperate."

"Well then, Mr. President. Why don't you name Gerald Ford Vice-President and then convince the Rockefellers that he won't run in 1976, and that you will support Nelson Rockefeller for the nomination and guarantee them you will get the Republicans to buy it."

President Nixon didn't look too happy with my suggestion. And after I left the White House, this feeling also left with me.

The Watergate break-in occurred June 17, 1972. Nixon and Agnew, five months later, won re-election in November 1972. The Watergate break in, true to Rockefeller's word, was not an issue. After the elections, criminal investigations commenced against Spiro Agnew, a sitting Vice-President of the United States. In August 1973, Spiro Agnew became the first Vice-President of the United States to resign from office.

President Nixon appointed Gerald Ford, not Nelson Rockefeller, Vice-President of the United States.

The Rockefellers justly acted as though Nixon stabbed them in the back. Watergate became the dominant daily news story of the land, and Nixon himself was now facing criminal indictment and impeachment.

The Rockefellers controlled the next deal. They told Nixon he would resign (in disgrace), and that Ford, who would move to President, would appoint Nelson Rockefeller Vice-President. The kicker was that Ford would pardon Nixon within thirty days; which the Rockefellers interpreted would preclude Ford from the Presidential nomination in 1976, since the country would refuse to vote for him. That would pave the way for Nelson. In this fashion, Nixon paid, and the Rockefellers would save face.

Ford immediately pardoned Nixon, to the anger of the Nation. To Nixon's credit, with nothing to personally gain, he did what he could to stop Rockefeller from finalizing his goal. He encouraged his fellow Republicans to give the 1976 nomination to Ford, even though Rockefeller was accurate that Ford would wind up losing the election, which he did in November 1976 to Jimmy Carter.

When Ford ran for the Presidency in 1976, Nelson Rockefeller did not want to run on the ticket as Vice-President, upset that his fellow Republicans would not listen to him that he, not Ford, could win in 76. Gerald Ford ran with Robert J. Dole. Nelson Rockefeller left politics in disgust and very angry. Consistent with Rockefeller integrity, however, Jimmy Carter won the Presidency in November 1976.

While I always wondered how history would have been different had President Nixon in 1973 appointed Nelson Rockefeller rather than Gerald Ford Vice-President, what has greatly disturbed me was Nixon's fear that he might befall the same fate as Kennedy.

The American public needs to know the truth of the Kennedy assassination because without the truth, it leaves the door continually open for forces and powers to exist in diametric opposition to the principles of our democratic constitutional government.

On January 26, 1979, Nelson Rockefeller died of a massive heart attack, in highly embarrassing circumstances, the least of it, being in the arms of his personal secretary, with whom he carried on an affair for many years. The stewardship of the Rockefeller family went to Nelson's youngest brother, David Rockefeller. *Regrettably for the country, David didn't need to win the Presidency in order to run it.* David Rockefeller would now pay back America for so malevolently treating his revered brother, Nelson.

CHAPTER 5
BRILLIANCE OF EVIL

When I was at law school in Washington, I had several good friends there from New York. These were long time friends, with whom I had grown up with in New York.

One of my closest was a real ladies' man, and on the day he first met his future wife I was there with them.

She was a very pretty gal, from one of Washington's leading families. This also meant that she was very rich and she lived close to my friend and me.

The very first night set the tone of the relationship. She drag raced against me and my friend up Connecticut Avenue. My friend wasn't going to lose to a woman, and she wasn't going to lose period. So rather than make this first meeting one in the local hospital, I cajoled my friend to let her win.

They were a great couple. I loved them. They loved me. The only problem was her parents. They hated my friend. He wasn't rich or cultured enough for their daughter, and they detested his complete attitude of independence. The parents, from the first, saw that there was no way they could ever control my friend, even with a short leash.

On the day they got married, the two families openly demonstrated intense dislike for one another. My friend's new wife had enough, and, after the wedding, she ceased her relationship with her parents, as she and her husband moved into an inexpensive apartment in Silver Springs, Maryland.

Now, this was a gal who didn't know what the inside of a kitchen looked like. This was a gal who grew up with everything and was denied nothing.

You wouldn't know it. Without much money between them to support the life-style she was accustomed to, she had to shop, she had to clean, and she had to forego restaurants and make dinner each and every night, not only for her husband, but for me too, each and every time I visited. But they were a happy and loving couple. I was so happy for my friend, and I loved his wife, because she had strength and character one could only admire.

All went well for more than a year. One night I heard from my friend that her parents wanted to repent. They wanted to accept him and have their daughter back in the family. They apologized profusely and asked them to move back into Washington D.C. They picked out a beautiful apartment in a great area of Washington and told my friend that they would not only pay the rent but also completely furnish it.

My friend asked me what I thought. I said, you and I both know a leopard doesn't change its spots. However, I said, one couldn't refuse such an offer, not the financial side, but he couldn't deny his wife the opportunity to recapture her family.

So he moved with his wife from a home of happiness to one of ruination and divorce, because none of us at such a young age could perceive the brilliant, full spectrum of evil.

What her parents did was a lesson forever forged into my mind. She was put in a building where all the wives were young wives with whom she grew up with; who married successful professionals or men from very wealthy families, who wore beautiful jewelry, had very expensive and luxurious fur coats, and who all traveled extensively with their husbands everywhere around the world.

What the parents were originally hoping for was that their daughter would revolt against cooking dinners, washing dishes and floors and living the life of a regular American wife in the early 70s. Now, they angled the situation where they hoped to emphasize that she married the wrong fellow because she couldn't compete with her former friends, where before, they couldn't compete with her.

What evil. The irony is that their plans didn't succeed with her: she loved my friend. They succeeded because he fell victim to their design, feeling inadequate, not being able to give his wife a shadow of what the other young wives in the building had from their husbands.

Her parents, while paying the rent and fully furnishing the apartment, offered not a cent more.

Their divorce made me sick then and still makes me sick today. But the lessons learned may have helped serve the Nation.

CHAPTER 6
1982

By 1982, my primary focus was on complex machine intelligent computer algorithms, rather than the law. This shift stemmed from a 1977 litigation against a Fortune 100 company, compelling me to learn everything about computers. What I learned is that I had an intense interest and talent for developing complex computer algorithms.

After discovering my new interest, I first attempted to develop algorithms, which would permit computers to comprehend language. I figured that whomever did develop the algorithm would rule the world. Once you can get a computer algorithm to understand language, you are at the embryonic stage of a computer system, which will ultimately write its own code.

Once computers write their own code, all that is in the world today is essentially no more. A completely new era opens, one dynamically totally different than the one we are in now, and one which will question man's role on the planet and highlight his limitations.

Nevertheless, I was fortunate enough to realize that my original goals were too ambitious and I set out to develop non-linear machine intelligent algorithms, which analyzed investment markets. I was very successful here.

The easiest way to show you the revolutionary new power created, and, to highlight, what was going on in the world in 1982, is by telling you that in August 1982, I started receiving newspaper coverage about some of the interpretations I was making at the time.

The *Courier Post* on August 29, 1982 wrote that despite predictions by Henry Kaufman of Salomon Brothers to the contrary, that interest rates fell from 16.5 percent to 13.5 percent, as I, Noah Guerin, had interpreted.

I think I stood alone in my interpretation. No one in 1982 opposed Henry Kaufman, the number one economic guru. Moreover, the situation in 1982 was very bleak: the U.S. was facing, at minimum, a serious recession and the possibility of a genuine full blown economic depression.

My personal perspective, when Ronald Reagan assumed the Presidency, in January 1981, was that he would allow a recession, as part of the cleansing process to the Presidential fiscal mismanagement since Johnson and the Vietnam War. President Reagan campaigned and was a hawk for a balanced budget. In 1982, interest rates had reached 16%, unemployment was at 11%, and the U.S. dollar was sliding in value – all due to the massive national deficits and debt.

The *New York Times* on August 8, 1982, carried a headline entitled "THE EROSION OF AMERICAN INDUSTRY. The recession's cruel effects are expected to cut deeply into business and the economy for many year to come." On August 9, 1982, I sent out to my new group of clients a special report, based on my machine intelligence, which supported a bull market, with dramatically lower interest rates and a stable to higher dollar.

This is how I made my mark and it was one of the earliest displays of machine intelligence for profit. It not only made my clients and me money, but it opened the door to a new dimension of geopolitical analysis.

Because while everyone thereafter witnessed the greatest bull market in world history, very few people knew the true reasons behind it.

Remember, my new computer intelligence not only told me about an imminent bull market, but also that the dollar would gain in value while interest rates collapsed.

How could that be? Jimmy Carter during his term in office between 1977 and 1981 was forced to increase interest rates to historical levels to protect against a collapse in value of the U.S. dollar.

Now, here I was saying that President Reagan was going to coerce the Federal Reserve to lower interest rates and under Reagan, contrary to Carter, the dollar would not only not collapse, as Jimmy Carter feared, but do the opposite, increase in value!

When the *Courier Post* reporter asked me how much further I expected interest rates to fall, I said the government agenda was to see interest rates move as low as possible. Over the course of the next decade, interest rates fell another ten percentage points; from 16.5 to 13.5 to under 3.5 percent!

The power represented by machine intelligence was awesome. Not only did it make me a lot of money, but also it changed my life. It permitted me to make geopolitical judgments and interpretations unheard of by a person working independently with a machine intelligent system.

It also was the basis for my getting called again to the White House, this time to meet President Reagan. But before I tell you about that, let me tell you why Reagan could do what Jimmy Carter couldn't do.

The only way that the U.S. Federal Reserve could move interest rates down, while keeping the dollar stable, was by receiving the cooperation of foreign countries. Little known by the American public, the leaderships of the seven leading industrial countries met in June 1982 to discuss coordinated economic policies. The countries were part of a group called the G-7; short for Group of Seven, comprised of the United States, Canada, England, France, Germany, Italy and Japan.

The central banks of the entire G-7 made an agreement allowing the U.S. to dig itself out of the higher interest rate hole. If this agreement wasn't reached, the *New York Times* gloom and doom headline may have very well become reality.

However, with central bank support from the leading industrial nations, the U.S. could lower interest rates gradually, without facing attacks on the dollar which would compel the Federal Reserve to raise interest rates, which would only further undermine then current concerns over the future for the U.S. greenback.

My friend, who had gotten divorced, remained in Washington, and as fortune and fate had it for me, he married a gal who worked in the Reagan White House. Her family was very close to President Reagan and she was forwarding my new work in machine intelligence to him.

He was impressed with what he had read from July to November 1982. However, he was particularly interested in what I wrote in December

1982, because of disagreement with his Vice-President over economic policy. I wrote in December 1982:

> "…As we discussed in July, without the cooperation of foreign governments and foreign central banks, lower interest rates were not possible. When interest rates began their decline in the U.S., foreign central banks quietly intervened to keep the U.S. dollar strong. However, I now exclusively interpret that our foreign allies, Japan included, took unfair advantage of the strategy agreed to at Versailles by the U.S. and its allies in June 1982. Our foreign allies not only kept the dollar strong, but permitted their own currencies to dramatically fall against the dollar in the very face of plummeting U.S. interest rates. **The weaker currencies of our foreign allies in conjunction with lower interest rates gave foreign exports an unfair edge which boosted foreign economies at the expense of the U.S. economy {emphasis in original}."**

When my friend's new wife, Susan, called me, telling me that President Reagan wanted me to visit with him at the White House, I was very pleased to go for more than one reason.

President Reagan won the Presidency in November, 1980, took office in January 1981, and on March 31, 1981, only three months later, he was nearly assassinated by John Hinckley, an individual personally known to the Bush family; the very family of George Bush, the Vice-President of the United States, who would have assumed the Presidency in 1981, if one of the many bullets fired by Hinckley had reached an intended mark.

After the shooting, Hinckley was quickly declared mentally incompetent and he was sent to a mental hospital and seemingly historical oblivion.

After this event, President Reagan subtly changed his position on many matters, including a balanced budget. Although he still spoke balanced budget, he ultimately created five times the budget deficits of Jimmy Carter, who he and the press criticized, without mercy, with reference to a $50 billion dollar deficit. Reagan was going to wind up running $250 billion yearly deficits!

However, before he came to run these deficits he called me into the White House. President Reagan was carrying doubts about what he was doing. George Bush, his Vice-President, and the man who could have been President in March 1981, carried none.

No more breakfasts with the President alone. Now, I found myself in the Oval Office with President Reagan behind the desk and Nancy Reagan and Vice-President Bush on opposite ends of a couch.

The President, as a friend of Susan's family, seemed to give me a warm welcome and applause for the type of work I was doing "...which I am sure made you a lot of money."

He admitted that he and the Vice-President were having differences regarding the higher dollar and he was aware of my visit to the White House years earlier.

I told the President that I wasn't so sure if my visit in 1973 was good for President Nixon.

Casting off my remark, he asked me why I thought the dollar was so strong.

Consistent with my style, I told him straight out that I thought the Japanese were taking unfair advantage of the apparent deal made by the U.S. to have its allies and their central banks support the dollar, as we lowered interest rates.

If we didn't lower interest rates, we would be in a depression or recession. However, I said I could not understand why, when the dollar should have been sinking, the dollar was soaring. This, I told the President, had material consequences because it would permit the Japanese to lower their U.S. prices, increase their U.S. market share, cut U.S. businesses' profit margins, ultimately unfairly forcing many U.S. manufacturers to go out of business.

Vice-President Bush was enraged at my inference that I thought that the Japanese were deliberately supporting an overvalued dollar. He made it clear to the President that without Japan we would be facing a depression. According to Bush, it was thanks to Japan that we had a robust stock market and expanding economy, and, most importantly, lower interest rates.

When I pointed out to the Vice-President that the Japanese were the primary beneficiaries and were going to be more so in the future, I knew he wrote me off for saying what I did, following his remark to the

President. Several newspapers had covered my input on the economy, and never again did anyone write another word about my work after my meeting with the President.

I said in reply to the Vice-President: "Let me put it this way, Mr. Vice-President. Keep your eye on the ball. I am saying that if I am right, the Japanese will continue to lower product prices, which will start putting large numbers of U.S. businesses out of business for good."

"What would you suggest then?" asked the President.

"You cannot allow the strength in the dollar against the Yen and other foreign currencies. The agreement should have been, if it wasn't, to keep all currencies at stable price levels. It is ridiculous to accept a stronger dollar when our interest rates are falling. We did the deal because we were worried that the dollar would tank if we brought interest rates down. The last thing anyone expected to see was this kind of strength in the dollar."

"He's got a point, George," President Reagan said to the Vice-President.

"You can't stop market forces." the Vice-President retorted.

"That's my point Mr. Vice-President," I said. "It's not natural market forces. It can't be. That's why the deal was made in the first place."

"We already have offsets in place," Bush stated.

"Do you mind if I ask what they are?" I asked.

Mr. Bush didn't answer.

"Tell him George," the President said after looking at Nancy Reagan who had not uttered a word, and who would not utter a word the entire meeting.

"We are going to have the Federal Reserve further monetize to offset the negative impact of increased imports and lower exports."

Bush was saying that he had directed the Federal Reserve to print money, create a series of bonds which we would buy from ourselves, to offset the massive amount of business and dollars moving overseas, as represented by the enormous trade deficits. The proceeds resulting from this monetization would be distributed inside the U.S. economy to help offset the impact of the trade deficit. This is what worsened rather than helped the overall U.S. debt picture.

This gave me the chance to get to an area that interested me.

"President Reagan, may I ask you a personal question?"

"You can ask, but I may not answer."

"President Carter ran a $50 billion deficit and you are running one many times more and if you don't lower the strength in the dollar you may run a deficit five times the deficit Jimmy Carter ran. However, while he was criticized, you are being lauded. While the stock market sank under Carter, it soars under you. While interest rates went to historical highs with Carter's $50 billion deficit, interest rates are moving down promoting a recovery..."

"Don't you get it, Guerin" Bush snapped at me. "We made a deal. Why do you think we are avoiding a depression? In a depression, the whole country would be under the gun. Now some businesses are, and after we recover we will straighten things out."

"Yes," President Reagan joined in, "people are happy and what kind of happiness would I bring to them if I had let the country slip into a deep recession or worse?"

Bush had won. So I said: "I hope I at least opened your eyes. If the Japanese keep lowering prices and capture massive U.S. market share and close down numerous businesses, including critical businesses to U.S. long term interests..."

"I was very happy Susan gave me those newsletters and you send them to me," the President interjected in conclusion.

"What kind of work do you do?" the Vice-President asked sensing whatever conflict he had with the President was now over.

"Machine intelligent computer algorithms."

"Computer expert, huh?" he responded.

"No, Mr. Vice-President, ...in pursuing potential avenues computer intelligence can be utilized."

"Do you think computer intelligence will play an important part in military armaments," the Vice-President asked, a little more relaxed now that his authority was fully restored.

"I think computer algorithms can in essence fight all wars and end all wars. Computer systems give any country the ability to destroy any other country. You can't stop the development of computer algorithms and once they are built into military systems, missiles and armaments, and linked into satellite systems, no one has a chance."

"How would you deal with this disturbing development?" Bush asked.

I thought for a moment and said: **"I would like to be the covert seller of all weapon systems which would incorporate hidden codes by which I could neutralize or control the weapons at will by satellite."**

Vice-President Bush stood up and approached me and said: "That's the best thing you said all day long. Is it possible?"

"For sure, Mr. Vice-President. With the programming and technological talent in this country, I would think it's absolutely possible."

When I left the White House I had little doubt of who was running the show. Many people thought Nancy Reagan had an overbearing influence on the President. It wasn't her, it was George Bush.

I want you to know exactly what I was thinking when I flew back home to New York. I was thinking that before Reagan was shot by Hinckley, Reagan was a staunch supporter of a balanced budget. I was thinking he was a man who thought that if the country went through a rough time, it would be a cleansing process, where we would all get through it together, and start afresh from the errors of the prior administrations in terms of handling the growing debt crisis of the nation.

Instead, I saw a man who had taken a new road and one which was more George Bush than Ronald Reagan.

I thought about what would be different if Reagan was assassinated, and George Bush was sworn in by default as President of the United States.

And I sadly concluded, little. I could plainly see that Ronald Reagan was following a course set by others, not by himself.

In 1996, thirteen years later, I came across a newspaper article in the *Dallas Morning News*, which touched upon the very things disturbing me in 1983. Why the sudden change in President Reagan? No one questioned it, no one addressed it, and I saw with my own eyes who was running things in the oval office: the man who would have been President had John Hinckley on March 31, 1981 been a little more deadly in his aim and mission.

Here's what the *Dallas Morning News* had to say, in part, in an article headlined *Dallas Council on World Affairs Thinks Globally, Acts Locally (05/12/96)*:

> The Dallas Council on World Affairs has not been hiding in the shadows since its founding in 1951.
>
> It has served as a forum for such world figures as Harry S.Truman, Hosni Mubarak, Yitzhak Shamir, Richard Nixon, George H.W. Bush, Boris Yeltsin, Jeanne Kirkpatrick, Henry Kissinger and others.
>
> But when internationally minded H. Neil Mallon brought his Dresser Industries from Cleveland to Dallas after World War II and created the council, provinciality was still the day. Dallas and Fort Worth didn't wish to share an international airport, much less a worldly vision.
>
> Yes, there were such local visionaries as Stanley Marcus, the recent recipient of the (Mrs. Clyde) Emery Award from the Dallas Committee for Foreign Visitors - a volunteer organization under the aegis of the council.
>
> Such groups were aware that ideas, art, finance and trade washed over national boundaries in the same fashion as the fashions of Paris and Milan.
>
> **In fact, the one-world views of Mr. Mallon, close friend of U.S. Sen. Prescott Bush of Connecticut and financial patron of Mr. Bush's son George's entry into the Midland oil industry,** even became suspect as Dresser's sales leaped the Iron Curtain and the McCarthy era found fertile soil in Big D.
>
> There was a noticeable rightward drift for some years discernible in the makeup of the staff and list of guest speakers, although the council prides itself on its forum for divergent views.

In recent years, under the guidance of Maj. Gen. Willard Latham as executive director, the council has maintained an even keel, faithful to its original mission.

With the advent of Dallas as an influential world city, the council is looking for ways to expand its horizons. No surprise when you consider that the current council president is an executive in a corporation whose operations and sales span the earth and was so important in the high-tech revolution.

He is Dr. Norman Neureiter, former U.S. diplomat and currently TI vice president-Asia, who returned not long ago from a stint in Japan and other Pacific Rim nations.

"I want to build on the rich legacy of this council, to stand on the shoulders of those who laid the foundation as we reach into the 21st century," he says.

Dr. Neureiter, who became president a year ago, adds, "I was really excited and enthused by the vision with which former Dallas Mayor (Annette Strauss) defined the city's role in the world. "We will make Dallas a great international city," a view adopted by mayors Steve Bartlett and Ron Kirk.

***

Dr. Neureiter, Mr. Holliday and the business, cultural and civic stalwarts of the council have great plans - to increase membership, increase the operating budget, institute a major fund drive, create an endowment and bolster programs that challenge and involve the lay public and local, national and world leadership alike.

If you wish to be a part of these plans, call the council at 748-5663 or its fund-raising auxiliary - **Les Femmes du Monde**, which holds a four-day event each September - at 350-4406.

Staff columnist Robert Miller writes about people and events of interest to the business community for The Dallas Morning News.

Les Femmes du Monde means "Women of the World." The first steps to deliberately dilute the honor and the name of the United States of America were being taken by George Bush during Ronald Reagan's tenure.

The Dallas Council on World Affairs, just like the Council on Foreign Relations, one of David Rockefeller's pet groups for a one-world order, was in control. If they could beat out a guy like Ronald Reagan, they could beat up and out a lot of other world leaders too. *The one world order required a fixed leadership in place.* I felt the danger in 1983 and subsequent years proved how correct those feeling were.

In the meantime, in 1986, *three years after my Oval Office meeting with Reagan and Bush,* without directly pointing to Japan, and after several years where Japan was declared the primary economic world power, and U.S. businesses were falling like flies to increasing Japanese quality and market share, *President Reagan announced an immediate need to reduce the strength in the U.S. dollar.*

And the Japanese with typical aplomb were totally prepared for President Reagan's announcement. They were the first to say that Japan, as a valued ally, would be in the forefront in cooperating with U.S. requests.

Commencing in 1986, the U.S. dollar weakened, as President Reagan requested, and, as a result, the Japanese nearly came to own us by buying up everything important in the United States. They were able to do this because President Reagan waited too long in seeking a weaker dollar.

Due to the Reagan sought weakness in the dollar, instead of the Japanese taking their U.S. dollar profits and converting them to previously inexpensive Yen, they kept their U.S. dollar profits in the U.S. and also now converted their Yen, accumulated during the 1982-1986 period, to cheap U.S. dollars. By doing so, they started buying up whatever quality businesses were left in America: from real estate to top technological companies.

They did just that, without shame or remorse, between 1986 and 1991.

CHAPTER 7
MISSING OUT ON A SUMPTUOUS DINNER

During my diplomatic law class in 1969 at the GW Law School, I also became friendly with many of the leading staff at the Chinese Embassy in Washington.

While their English was so-so, they were obsessed at learning about America and Americans. However, they were the product of their past and environment, and that being the case, gave me an early lesson in the late 60s of the major differences in cultures.

They invited me to dinner. We agreed to meet at the leading Chinese Restaurant in Washington.

As an American, I was expecting to meet up with them at the restaurant, sit at a table and have a meal with them.

Oh no. They arranged in advance, without my knowledge, for a private dinner in a private room at the restaurant that had several dishes ready and waiting for us.

The owner of the restaurant himself served us, and I, as the guest, got served first.

The first dish was pork.

I said no thank you.

They all to a man said no.

The next dish was lobster.

I said no thank you.

They all to a man said no. The leader of the group, spoke to the owner in Chinese.

The owner asked me why I was saying no.

I told him I was Jewish and didn't eat pork or lobster. I really wasn't sure whether he even understood; but, I discovered later on that my hosts didn't.

The next dish the owner served, my luck not panning out very well, was something else I didn't eat. When I said no, the entire contingency stood up, shouted at the owner, and stormed out of the restaurant.

I never saw them again: even at the class.

We, as Americans, think it presumptuous of others to order for us. They, as Orientals, thought it correct for them to order and could not for the life of them understand why I was saying "No." I, as an American, couldn't understand that even if I was saying "no" why they couldn't just simply say "yes" and eat the food themselves.

Further, to their minds, even if I wanted to say "no," I should have said "yes" and then not eaten it.

I was more upset why they couldn't tell me they were going to order all this stuff in advance, so I could tell them that I couldn't eat it.

The owner was nearly in tears and was so upset he wasn't able to comprehend any further explanation. I laugh at the whole thing now but, from this experience, I learned a lot about Asian cultures and moreover this served me, as did other experiences in Washington, for the important events to follow, years later, in New York.

New York in 1990 was an alive town, particularly if you received the right invitations. I did, and just being there introduced me to the movers and shakers of not only New York, but the world.

All these institutions I came in contact with would rent out various cultural centers and throw dinners and private performances for their top clients and invited guests.

One night, at one of these private galas in 1990, I met Nikko. She was the first woman to really move me since my brief encounter with Christine in Acapulco.

I should more accurately tell you that before I met Nikko I met her father, Nakusan Kaitu, who was having trouble with the FDA, the Food and Drug Administration, in getting approval for a revolutionary new type of sunglass from Japan.

He had told me that U.S. sunglass manufacturers were using government connections to make sure his sunglasses were not sold in the United States.

After he explained to me the nature of his sunglasses, and how they would for sure negatively impact U.S. sunglass manufacturers, I knew something was remiss.

He told me that he paid his attorneys over one million U.S. dollars over the past four years and they couldn't get the FDA to budge. For him, it was now or never and several people he knew recommended that he speak to me on how he could otherwise handle it.

At first, I thought he believed I was Italian and a member of the "U.S. Yakuza." In Japan, you had to pay off for everything, and he just wanted to know who he had to pay off. He was never able to get an answer.

I asked him who his attorneys were. He told me they were a firm I knew which also had offices in Washington, D.C. I told him to call them up and to arrange meetings with two Senators and two Congressmen who oversaw the FDA. I would then travel with him to Washington so we could meet with these Senators and Congressmen.

At the meetings in Washington, Nakusan sat there in stark fear of opening his mouth in manifest awe of sitting with me, directly talking, at the Capitol, with U.S. Senators and Congressmen. The one thing you learn in Washington is that these Senators and Congressmen are the very same guys who you got drunk with when you used to see them at the Washington parties. You just have to tell them where and when you saw them and they always are at their best to you, lest you tell them how stupidly they were acting when they were trying to manhandle the girls at the parties.

In any event, after two days of meetings, Nakusan was amazed. We got one of the Congressmen to say that the thing smelled and he was going to move on it.

The Congressmen's aid went so far as to tell Nakusan that he expected that they could have everything cleared up within three weeks at the latest.

Nakusan didn't know what to say or do. After four years, he saw real progress in two days.

He asked me what he should do. I told him that in America you support Congressmen who do the right thing. If he did the right thing, not per se because it was for his own interests, but in that competitors were using the FDA to do dirty work, and he was going to stop it, that he should support the Congressman by making a donation to him or his political party.

He asked how much.

I told him that he should consult with his regular lawyers, if and after we got good news.

I had to fly to Seattle and would you believe that he flew there with me just to keep me company. When we landed, he immediately boarded a return flight to New York.

Now that Nokki, his daughter, introduced herself to me at a function at the Metropolitan Opera House, at Lincoln Center, she told me she knew who I was and that her father spoke very highly of me.

First reactions are always chemical and the chemistry was there. And I knew that she would certainly join me after the opera for a night around town.

The difficult part was deciding whether to ask her up to my place. I really wanted to. She was captivating. After all the drinks and dancing we did, she also wanted to hear we were going to my place.

However, I just took her home. Since I knew her father, it would be disrespectful to him and his family had I not done so.

The next day, when she reflected on it, she was very happy we ended the evening as we did.

That only made things better for everyone because I suddenly was asked to do a lot of work for a lot of different Japanese people and firms in New York. I need not tell you who had the money in those days.

However, I took on very little work for the Japanese because my focus was on my machine intelligence research. Nokki and I would spend countless hours walking about Central Park talking about the implications for the U.S., Japan and the world of the continued computer revolution ahead. My memories are full of the discussions and the times we shared.

I found out she was from a leading Japanese family and that sunglasses were only a small part of it. Her father's three brothers ran a lot of major business out of Japan. I couldn't care less. What I cared about is what I remember so well: the night we consummated our relationship.

We had spent the day browsing all around Canal Street in lower New York and she picked up endless things at the market, taking them to my place near Wall Street to cook up a meal. Boy did she know how to cook. She could speak five languages. She could play three musical instruments. She could write in three languages. She would answer almost any question you could think of. She was warm and loving and caring. She was darn near perfect.

After dinner, Nokki and I went into the bedroom to watch my favorite movie: Daryl F. Zanuck's 1935 production of the Victor Hugo classic: *Les Misérables*.

I always felt that by looking at someone's reaction to this movie I could tell, in a short period of time, a great deal about the genuineness of the person.

It took nearly three months before Nokki and I watched the movie together.

Les Misérables involves the harsh ten-year imprisonment of a man, Jean Valjean, for stealing, when hungry, a small piece of bread.

When released from prison, he cannot find a place to sleep on a rainy down trodden evening. He is sitting on a public park bench, visibly ill and shaken and miserable after being turned away from every boarding house and door until a man crosses his path, hears his story, and asks the fellow: "Have you tried the door over there?" pointing to a house by the church.

The released prisoner, who was a man without religious conviction whatsoever, was so desperate, he did try the door. He was invited in not for a simple meal but a sumptuous one, with expensive silverware laid out by the direction of the Bishop, who was the man who had spoken to him in the park, and in whose home Valjean now found himself a guest.

Jean Valjean eats as he hasn't for years and has a tormenting night's sleep, at the Bishop's house, as all the tensions from the years of physical and mental abuse come to the forefront of his sleeping conscious.

He awakes in anger and leaves the premises taking with him two expensive silver candlesticks. He could be seen as a clear-cut ingrate, who deserved the life of misery he suffered.

He is stopped by police officers who inspect his marked passport as a released prisoner and when they see the two expensive candlesticks, they arrest him. He tells them, in desperation and in sheer terror of being once again imprisoned, that the Bishop gave them to him.

They return to the Bishop's house and when the police officers confront the Bishop with what the released prisoner told them, the Bishop acknowledges Valjean's story! Jean Valjean in sheer shock stands in awe of his first blessing in life, as an aura of good fortune befalls him.

When the police officers leave, the Bishop tells Valjean that the candlesticks, as property of the church, belong to him as much as they do to the Bishop. He says to take them; to remember the day's events, and to use them in the spirit of the day.

Jean Valjean returns on his unknown path with an aura to repay the Bishop for his good deed. He finds God and vows to help others as the Bishop helped him.

This first phase of the story, as portrayed by the 1935 movie, is extremely powerful and touching.

When President Reagan after the assassination attempt, changed his policy of dealing with our economic problems, he sidestepped the principle that it is in times of adversity that we are at our best, and develop and show the greatest kindness towards our fellow man.

In adverse times of military battle, rich and poor, regardless of class or station in life, work and operate together for common interests: a poor man will act to save the life of his rich comrade, as will a rich man act to save the life of a poor man, regardless of whether his future seems less valuable than his. It is the bonds and experiences gained in times of adversity, which plant the seeds of a new generation of men of character and commitment. By avoiding adversity, and just assuring everyone happiness and glee, a new generation has no reference for appreciating what they have and from where they came.

Jean Valjean knew from whence he came, and he knew the injustices suffered. He spent his life working towards the commitment of improving the lives of others less fortunate. The Bishop's good deed and blessing permitted him to build a successful company, first financed by those silver candlesticks. He worked day and night to make that business a success so that he would have the ammunition, the resources, to honor his pledge to the Bishop, to himself and to God.

Nokki seemingly was openly moved with every twist and turn of the movie. She held me tight and before the movie was over looked in my eyes, as we both realized we were both of similar mind and disposition toward what we had already seen and where we were headed.

The beauty and happiness of the evening was not to last long.

I loved Nokki. No two ways about it. And her family openly loved me, or it seemed that way, until several months later, when Nakusan said he wanted to have dinner with me and several distinguished guests coming to New York from Tokyo.

I asked him who they were and he simply said to be at the Ushio Restaurant at 9:00 PM Wednesday evening.

Perhaps private dinning rooms are not a good omen for me. For sure this one on Wednesday evening, on East 49th Street, was not.

Nakusan, in front of his guests, acted as though he was honoring me by introducing them to me. His actions and words further suggested that he was also honoring me by telling me that they wanted me to represent them in a sensitive matter in the United States.

There were three men visiting and they were from the three main Japanese chip manufacturers in Japan. They wanted the doors opened to Japanese chips in the United States. The U.S. was protecting Intel and other U.S. chip manufacturers from the type of competition, which drove U.S. businesses down the tubes, and critical high tech businesses into Japanese investment portfolios. The U.S. could not be dependent on foreign firms for computer chips.

I thought the U.S. position was correct. So I simply told these men that I would not represent them because, diplomatically put, I had a conflict of interest. I hinted that I had clients in the chip manufacturing business in the U.S. and my representation of them would create an inherent conflict of interest.

Nakusan wasn't very happy when I said this. However, he was prepared. He said that I should drop all these clients and these men will pay me triple the total billing of all these other clients combined.

I didn't like the attitude that Nakusan displayed in so telling me. He was always warm and friendly and now that infamous guard dog was coming back into the forefront of my mind.

I couldn't understand why Nakusan didn't ask me first whether I would have any reservations about representing such an issue. I concluded that for some reason he assumed I had strong enough contacts to help overturn a major government policy.

So I said, to put an end to the entire matter: "Gentlemen, I also have a relationship with the U.S. government which forbids my involvement in such a matter. A relationship I cannot discuss."

Was I surprised in what came next. Nakusan said directly: "We are aware that you have met with Reagan and Bush. My honored guests represent some of the biggest interests in our country. They have in their pocket a check for $1,000,000, as a down payment for your services, if you find yourself a way to represent their interests and take this matter up with President Bush. They believe a change in policy is beneficial to the United States and they are willing to explain it to you."

I didn't like the entire thing. I didn't like the pressure, the money, the knowledge that they knew I had met with Reagan and Bush: especially when the only people who knew about it from me were my friend and his wife, Susan. I never told Nikko anything about Reagan, Bush or Nixon.

I wanted out of there: "Nakusan, I normally undertake representation of issues I personally support. When you were wronged about your sunglass business, I represented you and helped correct the situation. I cannot help correct a situation that I personally believe is a correct policy on the part of the United States.

"If this compromises your honor with these men, my regrets. However, it would be a waste of your time and their time if I gave any impression except for the one which will ultimately result from our discussion."

One of the three men was particularly displeased. He through Nakusan said that a lawyer represents interests regardless of his personal beliefs concerning those interests. He said I should take the money and whatever I did for them would be acceptable.

This was very clever of him and showed how well they knew my personality. From whom? Nikko? I could never take so much money and not do something for them. I knew I didn't want to represent them on this issue, so I politely declined.

When I next saw Nikko I knew that my name lost a lot of its luster in her household. I didn't want to get into it but I did say to her that if her father had asked me in advance about the issue, I would have told him what my position would be and avoided whatever embarrassment resulted that evening to him.

Nikko then said something that did not foreshadow well. "Noah-san," as she called me, "in life you have to make decisions as to who are your friends and future family. My father introduced you to three of the most powerful men in Japan. If you represented them, whether successful or not, you would have aligned yourself and helped my family further entrench itself with the most powerful group of people in our country.

"Not only did you have a window to grasp an opportunity rarely open or available, but you had the chance to further our relationship and future together."

I said: "Nokki, I don't understand why this meeting has anything at all to do with our own personal relationship. Whether I can help your father in his interests should have nothing to do with what is between us."

"This is not so Noah-san," Nokki said. "I must tell you now something which will upset you more than you have upset my father."

If she was going to tell me that she wouldn't see me any more, then she wasn't the gal I thought she was all along. She did far worse.

"I will be leaving the United States next week to marry."

"Marry who?" I asked in astonishment.

"A man I have never met, Noah-san," Nokki said. "It is a political marriage to the son of someone high up in the Korean government. This will be beneficial to my family."

I thought I was going to get sick in front of her. "I thought your family is wealthy, Nokki. Why is it so important to increase their power or position with a marriage to someone you haven't even met. This, Nikko, of course, is aside from the fact," I said with some sarcasm, "that perhaps you want to marry someone you love and know; not to say writing off everything that exists between us."

Since the time we watched *Les Misérables*, Nokki and I both felt a serious bond between us, one where we entertained the thought of marriage. Now, she was coldly telling me to my outright dismay that our discussions would prove to be nothing better than an illusion.

She explained to me that in Japan her commitment to her family's interests superseded everything. Her family, while rich, had to also maintain and increase political power to protect what they had in the family, passed on through many generations. So, if I had represented these dominant businesses in Japan, her father, or better said, her family's interests, would be protected and her father and family would have added honor and power.

Now, that I had declined what she referred to as "this extraordinary opportunity," her father, and her family's interests were weakened, and she had to do, as her father arranged, as an alternative: an important political marriage to a leading South Korean family.

Aside from everything you yourself are thinking, I pointed out to Nokki that I thought the Japanese weren't particularly fond of Koreans. She simply said that they weren't but that this is what she had to do.

I was going to ask her one more thing before leaving for the nearest bar: why she didn't tell me the consequences of my decision before the meeting.

However, it didn't matter any more. I was up against a different culture and that guard dog came back again and again in my mind. Could Nokki ever love me more than the tradition of serving her family? I didn't know, and I didn't care.

I was very upset and depressed about the entire thing for a long time. No one could cheer me up, and, even today, more knowledgeable about the Japanese than ever before, I find it difficult to believe that her personal feelings for me would be overridden by an aberrational demand to marry a man she never met.

In my dreams, the guard dog lunged at me. The Chinese were leaving the restaurant again and again.

All the beauty, excitement and passion of Nikko were no more. Nikko was lost to me.

CHAPTER 8
$1000 BET

Since I trust you would be as upset as I was in what happened with Nikko, I want to tell you, as soon as possible, that I met with George Bush in late 1991, and one of the first things the President told me was that Nakusan Kaitu was a U.S. operative.

Nakusan was acting in that capacity for the United States in my 1990 meeting, and, because of that meeting, Bush lost a $1000 bet to Reagan, since Bush was betting Reagan that I would take the million-dollar check.

I didn't, and earned the reluctant respect of Bush. After I met with him in late 1991, I have to tell you he didn't earn any respect from me.

Before I forget, I asked Bush whether Nikko was knowledgeable about her father and whether she too was an agent. Her entire relationship with me would then have been artificial.

I didn't want to guess what the answer would be.

President Bush told me that Nikko had no idea. Nakusan was one of their best-placed operatives and his daughter didn't know anything. Nakusan, he said, was now dead since some one deep in the CIA sold the Japanese data revealing that Nakusan worked for us.

I then asked him about Nikko. President Bush told me she was married to the Korean and while avoiding telling me her husband's relationship with the United States, he told me clearly that she was stuck in that relationship for the rest of her life. Subject to Korean law, in terms of her marriage and relationship with her husband, she had no way out. His family was supremely powerful in Korea, and he told me not to think about looking for Nikko.

I didn't tell the President, but I didn't want her because I couldn't accept her willingness to do what she did to me in the past, and the way she did it was even worse.

The President, however, sort of suggested, that my thinking may have been wrong about Nikko. He asked me why did I turn down the million dollars. He said I could have represented them legally and established a financial cow for my future, which may have included Nikko. I think he was telling me that he would have taken the money.

The President, knowing from the FBI and IRS, how I was doing financially when I saw him, said I could have been a very wealthy man worth tens of millions of dollars.

He said to me that I should snap out of it because even though he knew I was doing well in my business, that I rarely advertised and that my business should be at least ten times bigger than it was then for what I had to offer. He asked me whether I was still depressed over Nikko. I guess he also knew that I hadn't formed a relationship with anyone that lasted more than three days, or better said three nights.

"You know Noah, the guys here can never figure out what you are going to do. You're really unpredictable."

"I can't be bought. Does that make me unpredictable?"

"No, it's that you don't seem to react to money and power the way everyone else does. Do you mind telling me why?"

"Before I tell you, Mr. President. Tell me one thing. If I took the million dollars, and my now knowing that Nakusan was on your string, would you have set me up so that I was under your thumb too?"

The President smiled. "All I will say Noah is that you would have been in a position to help us."

"Who's the us, Mr. President. CIA, DIA, Defense..."

"Everyone."

"I'm glad you lost the bet then."

Bush and his cronies, particularly, at State and the DIA, would have pushed Nakusan, perhaps as my father-in-law, to set me up to do something improper and then they would have owned me, flaunting a criminal prosecution over my head.

Now that they didn't succeed, I was free to be me and to one day try to stop the terrible course America was on, as you will soon see, as I relay to you why George Bush brought me to the White House.

CHAPTER 9
MONEY

I was thinking, after the President asked why I had not taken the money, about Nakusan being a U.S. operative and about his being used by President Bush, not to win a bet, but to set me up, where I would have no choice but to work for the government.

I also was thinking about my volunteer work at the Harkness Pavilion at Columbia Presbyterian Hospital in New York when I was a kid. All the rich New Yorkers came there in the 50s for treatment, and many came to die.

I thought about a particular experience that taught me a lot about life, and which experience some how propelled me to refuse the million-dollar offer.

When I was an early teenager, I was helping out the nurses in the ICU unit. One very rich fellow was losing ground in his battle for life when two twenty year olds walked in to see him, their father.

I saw one of the boys constantly in front of the mirror combing his hair and the other was standing there staring at his father, saying nothing.

In about, I would estimate, five minutes, and for sure less than ten minutes, the boys left. There was absolutely no emotion between them and their father.

Five minutes later the wife came in with a cake. It was her husband's 67th birthday. His wife asked where were her two boys. A nurse told her that they left. Several nurses and I joined the wife in singing him happy birthday. He died in the middle of the song.

It was such a moving moment, seeing a man die from sheer sadness.

The real meaning of the day came when I spoke about the event to other rich sick men at the hospital. They all had things in common: totally occupied by their professions and businesses, and by the time they could stay still for a moment, they were at the hospital sick or dying.

They had no relationship with their children. They provided their wives and children with everything but themselves. The essence of their talents and abilities they gave to their professions and businesses and then suddenly, since they were stuck at the hospital sick and dying, for the first time, they seriously assessed their lives.

What made the assessment easy was seeing everyone in their family fighting over their estates. No one cared about them, they were all fighting about who was going to get what. All the love and sincerity was a facade for learning what was going to be left to the actor or actress who usually was the wife, or a daughter, or a son, or brother, or nephew or cousin.

Most of the men came to realize that I, a mere volunteer, who had no connection at all with them, probably cared more about them than anyone in their own families.

They soon realized that if they would die tomorrow that all they worked so hard for would be a meaningless speck of dust in the spectrum of life. What they should have focused on was spending time with their children so there would be a relationship and love and caring and someone to properly manage what, if anything, they had built during their lifetimes. For most people, it was their name and reputation and who, and, what they stood for during their lives.

Now, they recognized much of their estates would be squandered away. That so many rich people came to realize this, proved quite beneficial to many of the charitable institutions in New York.

However, the people to blame for the misery were themselves. And they all knew it. Why did it take illness and death to bring clarity to their minds and life? I never could answer that until later in life when it became apparent most of us are taken in with the temptations of life. The million dollar checks, the invitation to join those in power, misdirects us from developing a life style, so that when we do go to the hospital and face death, we are proud about the lives we lived. Only in one instance did I see a very wealthy home that was also a happy home.

Thus, million dollar checks, particularly for the privilege of being held on a leash, was not an attractive proposition for me.

CHAPTER 10
POWER

The other aspect of President Bush's question related to what Nikko referred to: aligning yourself with power.

Power is vastly more important than money.

One day when in the Palm Beach area of Florida, I one day witnessed a conversation between two men arguing about their comparative success in terms of dollars and cents.

One said he was worth $168 million dollars. The other laughed and said he was worth $850 million dollars.

The point to my mind was that money above a certain level is meaningless. Each would never spend a fraction of the money he had. So what value did it have but to spoil their families and make problems rather than happiness prevail?

Very little, except to also confirm that the U.S. dollar wasn't worth much. What happened to the days that few even had a million dollars?

The real story of ambition and intrigue connects with power.

When you are poor, you only think of making money. When you have made a lot of money, you realize that money is nothing in comparison to power.

So President Bush's question also involved the dynamic of power. Even if I could step aside from $1,000,000, how could I step aside from alignment with Japan who in 1990 were the key players in the world and who would have seemingly provided me with a life of limitless opportunity and pleasure, including Nikko.

My answer to him was that:

> 1) As an American, I did not care to represent the Japanese against a major U.S. policy, which I supported;

2) I did not wish to forego my association with other clients to be an exclusive agent for a foreign country simply based on consideration of money;

3) power didn't interest me except where it could be used constructively and the Japanese weren't known for using it in such fashion;

4) I don't like being under the control and created environment of others, as it reminded me of my friend in Washington, who went from a simple home of happiness to an elegant home of ruination and divorce and;

5) I had my own interests in computer intelligence and other areas that I would have had to forego to exclusively give my time to those who offered me money and power.

Of course, I also added that now I also well knew it would have made me a prisoner of the U.S. government, as Bush would have pulled my strings as puppet master. **Many people fall into this role because of the attraction for money and power: how lucky are we who can find the strength to side step temptation. Most of us do not know to what degree we are blessed by our decision, a decision derided and seen by others as totally flippant and foolish.**

President Bush's question and my answer created the perfect tension for a fight that was still to erupt between us. You see, once you have power, as did President George H.W. Bush, the worse crime in life is to misuse it, or worse, abuse it.

CHAPTER 11
SPLIT IN THE ROAD

After President Bush finished making amenities with me, by bringing me up to date with Nikko and her family, we got down to the reason I was there.

It seems that during the course of his Presidency, President Bush determined that all I had told him in early 1983 was true. Japan wasn't really a cooperative member of the "family of nations," but a country with a hidden agenda to ultimately undermine U.S. interests. And they were doing a good job of it.

In October, 1991, the Japanese appointed a hard-liner to become premier. The first thing the new premier said was that Japan wasn't going to simply accede to everything the U.S. wanted and expected.

The powers in Japan were intent on distancing themselves from U.S. political interests. The *New York Times* on October 16, 1991, reported that Japan has coined a new word to reflect their sentiment toward America: "Kenbei." The article described the word as meaning a "dislike of the United States... there is a growing feeling that on trade issues, the United States is bullying Japan arrogantly making demands on every trivial matter that does not comply with the American standard of justice...Those on the U.S. side are still leaning heavily on Japan, never reflecting on their own country's shortcomings...And those on the Japanese side are still bowing before American demands, as if doing so was Japan's fate."

Japan was the supreme economic power in the world in 1991 and with it came arrogance. I know. I had enough Japanese clients.

When I told my Japanese clients that Japan should assess its current day obligations towards America by remembering that America allowed it to rebuild after WWII, and that if Japan won, the same would not have been true, their response angered me.

They told me that Japan could not be faulted for refusing to be as weak and foolish as America. To them, America made a foolish decision and it must now live with it. I said "thanks" and literally broke off relations with nearly all my Japanese clients at that time.

The Democrats just before my meeting with the President in late 1991 made several brilliant maneuvers, including beating Bush to a very popular capital gains suggestion and forcing Bush to cede on extending unemployment benefits. This type of maneuvering showed a new high-level strategic planner behind the Democrats, and when later on Bill Clinton entered the picture with Ron Brown, an open favorite of the Japanese power structure, all seemed very clear to me.

President Bush asked me whether I thought the Japanese were going to covertly support the Democrats and were likewise behind his recent setbacks.

"Yes, I do sir."

"I am going to go to Tokyo to put a stop to it, Noah. You were right all along about the Japanese. Amazing...

"But now Noah I want to know from someone who has been so darn right about so many things whether you think it wise I go and moreover is it safe for me?"

"Mr. President I don't think it would be either wise or safe for you. I think it would show weakness and desperation to the Japanese."

"So how can I change things?"

"That's a big question, Mr. President. Can I speak freely about my perceptions about your Presidency?"

"I have been reading what you have been telling your clients," the President admitted to me.

I told the President, I didn't realize I was sending him any of it, but, I guess, he was telling me he was reading everything I was sending to my clients via government snooping of electronic mail. That was the way I was communicating with clients in those days.

"In my opinion, they have determined that you are working to uproot the current power structure in Japan, Mr. President, and they are right about that. You can't blame them for fighting back."

"You said, Noah, it was you, wasn't it, that said they started things back in '82 by taking advantage of our request for lower interest rates?"

"I did, Mr. President, but if I saw right through what you did in Russia with Gorbachev, I wouldn't be connecting it to retaliation for what Japan has been doing for the past decade here. I would be connecting it with a U.S. agenda to take over."

What I was saying to President Bush was that without Gorbachev there would have been no break up of the Soviet Union. He was the ultimate friend of America and peace, because he was the catalyst for nuclear disarmament. This is why he was *Time Magazine's Man of the Century* and recipient of the Nobel Peace Prize. When Japan saw that the U.S. could turn on Gorbachev when he refused to fully abide by the U.S. agenda for the Soviet Union, the only conclusion to the Japanese was that the U.S. had short memories for "friends," and the true U.S. agenda was complete control. While the U.S. one day might pretend to argue with Tokyo about trade or some other matter, the true aim, to their minds, would be dominance and control.

"I really can't talk much about that with you, Noah."

"Well Mr. President if you can't talk much about it, I can't be of much help, unless you want me to make assumptions?"

President Bush showed how desperate he was when he told me to go on and make assumptions. He called me in because he wanted to hear my thoughts.

"First, of all you took out Gorbachev. This guy was the single reason for the break up of the Soviet Union and the defeat of Communism. Then you take him out and put in Yeltsin. Do you think you really fooled anyone?

"And Mr. President, I know who Gorbachev has to thank for being alive. President Reagan wouldn't be able to sleep knowing that the U.S. took him out after all Gorbachev did. Am I right?"

"Noah," the President interjected, "What would have happened if hard line Communists resurfaced after the break up? Gorbachev was willing to reshape Russia, but only up to a point, and then he was totally aloof to the dangers of taking it only so far and then letting the country get into the wrong hands.

"After the Iraqi war, what was I faulted on?" the President asked me rhetorically. "Wasn't it that I didn't finish the war by taking out Saddam?"

"Yes."

"And do you know why I couldn't take that pig out?"

"No, Mr. President."

"Because Gorbachev felt he had to kowtow to other Soviet political figures who said Russia owed it to Iraq and itself to protect Iraq from further U.S. intrusions. We got Saddam out of Kuwait, 'that's it,' they said. They wanted to show they still had some balls left and I was compelled to call it quits.

"Now, not only do I get the heat for making what looks to everyone like a stupid decision, but I can't even explain it.

"If Gorbachev wasn't taken out in August, I would have faced a far worse situation than Iraq."

I knew what President Bush was saying. He felt that if Gorbachev lost his hold over Russia that in view of the economic upheaval, the extremists would take over the country, would pose a supreme threat to world peace, and he would get the blame for mishandling it, as he did with the final phase of the war with Iraq. He wasn't going to mess up twice, at least in the minds of the general public and history books.

However, what disturbed me was that Gorbachev got the Nobel Peace Prize and was named *Time Magazine's Man of the Century.* Gorbachev became the entire catalyst for a new era of world peace and nuclear disarmament.

"Wasn't there a way you could work things out through Gorbachev, Mr. President?"

"We had a three day summit in Malta, Noah, in 1989. I pleaded with him to follow any one of a number of paths. Believe me, Noah, he lost touch with the situation. He did great in taking it so far, but there would have been WWIII or worse if we didn't take control of the situation. With all those nuclear weapons and warheads...and all those extremists around, it could have turned into a disaster."

President Bush was telling me that primary U.S. policy and interests had no alternative.

"However, you scared the Japanese and others including myself."

"Well now you know."

"But Mr. President, there's all this other stuff going on in England, Italy, France, and it's not stopping in Russia."

President Bush got somewhat red in the face. "The dangers we have in Russia apply to other countries as well."

The President for the first time confirmed to me that his agenda encompassed control over allied industrial nations. The same type of control the U.S. established in many third world countries.

"Here is where I am concerned, Mr. President, and quite frankly, Mr. President this is why I believe the Japanese situation is not resolvable by you. This is also the reason, Mr. President, why I believe the Japanese will not make any deal with you, to answer your question. Of course, I may be wrong, and you have intelligence I don't have."

"You seem to be doing very well with what you have, Noah," the President complimented me.

I was getting a little hot under the collar because I was now stepping on the concerns he admitted reading about in my transmissions to my clients. In the transmissions, I was critical of perceived U.S. policies.

"Mr. President, when the Berlin Wall fell you said that the world needed a "new world order." Am I entitled to hear what you have in mind?

"Mr. President, don't tell me anything that is even close to being classified. I don't want you to ask me to curtail what I say or do because I am privy to anything secret."

"You are a shrewd one, Guerin" the President responded. "Do you understand that what is going on today is outside the pale of most Americans' ability to understand?"

"What I understand Mr. President is that you are on a course to hand select leaderships in countries throughout the world. And I don't agree with that policy. I don't think it is within our right to do it and I don't think the American people would support it, if they knew about it."

Bush got angry. "Let me ask you this," he said with a changed tone of voice. "Remember when I asked you in 1983 regarding imbedded secret software programs?"

I wanted to beat the President to the punch. *"Yeah, you used it on the Sunday evening **nationally televised** air raid on Iraq."*

"How did you know that?"

"Look Mr. President, this covert U.S. policy Nixon told me that keeps Americans occupied with sports all weekend long has been a major success.

It is difficult to believe that Americans couldn't figure out that as stupid as they think Arabs are that even a child shooting missiles at random in the sky would have shot down more American aircraft."

Hundreds of U.S. aircraft were flying directly into Baghdad, with the Iraqi's shooting multiple anti-aircraft at these hundreds of aircraft. First, when only a few aircraft were lost, and second, when you see the U.S. nationally televise an event, where hundreds of U.S. servicemen could be killed on prime time live television, you know that the government knows the results in advance.

"Bravo!" Bush declared.

"Please, don't applaud me, Mr. President. If Americans weren't encouraged to be couch potatoes over exercising their minds on their time off, they would have realized that either this was an extraordinary piece of good fortune that more planes weren't shot down, or some other dynamics must have been in place."

"Believe me," the President said, "no one knows because they can't fathom the degree of sophistication our military weapons and strategic systems have today. Noah, if I turned off the TV for an entire year, the American public would never have figured it out!"

"I don't think you give them enough credit, Mr. President. Moreover, *they rely on government and especially the press and media to act as catalysts on the direction they should be thinking*. And President Nixon's prediction to me on that was also correct: he said I would discover one day that all the newspapers and media in this country were in limited hands and under the thumb of the government."

I continued: "What you can't tell me is what I already know, President Bush. That it is all part and parcel of the plan to implement this new world order. Now, that you used the words, you think you sanitized the concept. The American people are being kept in the dark about it."

"Without it, we cannot guarantee Americans peace and security. With it, Noah, we have our best chance to protect American interests."

"Like NAFTA, Mr. President?"

"What objection do you have to a global economy?"

"You are selling out Americans. You are moving not only to global trade but to a global currency and a centralized world order government. One where the candidates are only among those allowed to even run."

"You're talking nonsense."

"No I am not. Otherwise, you wouldn't have your fingers in every country's elections."

"Noah, I can use you and you belong with us. I've got my hands full with the Japanese and I would want you with me when I travel to Japan."

"Does my traveling with you mean that I am restricted from covering certain things in my transmissions to clients or ever writing a book about it."

"Yes."

"Mr. President. I have always been honored beyond words for the opportunity to give you and other Presidents my thoughts on a number of things. I have never sought anything. I consider it an honor and a public service. But I prefer to never get involved in anything which restricts me from speaking, acting or doing what I want to say or write about as an American citizen."

"I am asking you to come to Japan with me."

"I am saying no, Mr. President, unless you guarantee me the right to continue saying, writing or doing whatever I please as an American citizen."

"Good luck to you then," the President said in closing, standing up to shake my hand warmly.

CHAPTER 12
BUSH SHOULD HAVE STAYED IN WASHINGTON

I t wasn't I, however, who needed the first stroke of luck. It was President Bush.

Bush completely lost his eyes and ears in Japan. Due to the CIA mole, not only was Nakusan uncovered in Japan, but the entire U.S. network was out of business.

Bush made the biggest mistake of his entire career by going to Tokyo. And after it was over, he was glad to be alive, and all he could think about was that it was I who warned him not to go and that he should have listened to me.

It's hard to go after someone who tried to save you from the misery experienced during what was nothing less than a nightmare for George Bush.

The President thought he was going to go to Tokyo to push the Japanese around. What he got was insult at every turn, with the Japanese parading a monkey around named after him. America was derided without stop, and Bush received no cooperation whatsoever.

Such hostility was made no secret from the media. The *New York Times* on January 10, 1996, reported:

> "*Bush's Painful Trip.* There was no specter of nuclear war, of course. But negotiators seemed to realize that if the huge and growing trade deficit between Japan and the United States was not brought under control, it could drive Tokyo and Washington apart, hurt their economies *and damage Mr. Bush's re-election prospects.*...It was too early to discern the American political effects of the Tokyo talks. *But the widespread view in Japan was that the negotiators' efforts would not help the American economy or Mr. Bush's political fortunes,* and indeed that they could lead to even deeper Japanese-American antagonism.*"

During a formal State dinner for President Bush in Tokyo, he keeled over and vomited right at the table.

Aside from this having to have been a cosmic embarrassment for President Bush, it indicated to me that Bush was poisoned by the Japanese. Nikko had told me all about the Japanese expertise in poisons.

George Bush who one year before was a shoe-in for re-election and who had the highest popularity ratings imaginable, saw everything really go downhill for him after his return from Tokyo.

He ultimately received criticism from his own friends and cabinet in how he handled his campaign. What his close friends and political allies and he himself may not have understood is what happened to him.

We Americans perceive poisoning as something which makes someone violently and fatally ill moments or shortly after the ingestion of the poison. The Japanese, on the other hand, see poisoning as not only a tool for murder but as a delivery system of a special effect or result to the victim.

To them, if one ingests something and he loses his drive and ambition, where before he had drive and ambition, this would be tantamount to a successful poisoning. That is what happened, I believe, to the President.

The Japanese were positive that Bush would undermine the current Japanese power structure immediately after his re-election. They saw what he did to the Soviet Union and to "U.S. friend" Gorbachev. So Bush was Public Enemy Number 1. They treated him with disrespect, and his collapse at the dinner table, his heaving, his later loss of Presidential ambition and drive, was no surprise to me. He really should have listened to me. He could never fully understand the Japanese mindset, and if he did, he would have known that they were as fixed in their course as those behind Bush were set in theirs.

David Rockefeller told George Bush, after his election loss to Bill Clinton, that the Japanese would one day pay dearly for what they did to his friend.

When *Time Magazine* reported him a failed President (Is Clinton Up to the Job?), on its front cover in June 1993, during his first 100 days in office, he was open to and received assistance from those who took Clinton onto the tracks of the Bush "new world order.".

Clinton only had one goal. To win in 1996. His new team told him what to do and he did it. His popularity soared and David Rockefeller smiled.

Clinton was the best soldier yet for the Bush coined "new world order" agenda. During his first term, he put his fingers into politics and elections all over the world. He also went to war with Japan, the bad boy in the "family of nations." As a result, open hostility broke out between the countries.

The hostility was not fought on the military battlefield. It was fought by Japan trying to align the "family of nations" against the United States. They were forging deals and at that time most people thought Japan had the upper hand.

I did too.

With Clinton in office, the Japanese launched a major attack on the U.S. dollar, where the greenback sank to historical lows against all major foreign currencies. The Japanese, in my opinion, as I advised clients, were attempting to get the Yen to replace the U.S. dollar as the international currency of choice.

Aside from all major commodities, like oil, in the future being priced in Yen rather than dollars, the U.S. losing the dollar as the international reserve currency, would uncover all skeletons inside the U.S. dollar closet and put the U.S. into economic and financial chaos. The only reason the U.S. could get away with murder, in the way it handled its multi-trillion dollar national debt, is because the U.S. dollar was the international reserve currency. Now, with the dollar losing value by leaps and bounds, the Japanese were ready to launch their final attack.

And this is what exactly happened.

The U.S. wasn't getting anywhere with Japan. The dollar in 1993, 1994 and 1995 was getting hit all over the place and the U.S. knew who was behind it.

So in May, 1995, after the U.S. determined what the Japanese were doing, and after getting insulted by the Japanese in trade talks during all of 1994, the U.S. imposed harsh trade sanctions on Japan, effective June 28, 1995.

During most of 1994, the U.S. was threatening sanctions and the Japanese were laughing. Now, the U.S. intended to show Japan that it meant business.

The U.S. position is seen by a May 25, 1995, Reuters news report, excerpted below:

> SINGAPORE - Nearly two weeks after declaring that it would impose harsh trade sanctions on Japan, the Clinton administration is finding itself isolated and outmaneuvered around the world, with Asian governments joining their counterparts in Europe in condemning Washington's move to impose $6 billion in punitive tariffs against Japanese-made luxury cars.
>
> The sharp rejection of President Clinton's initiative in both Asia and Europe has come as a pleasant surprise to Japanese officials, and it seems to be emboldening them to face down the United States.
>
> ...Indeed, American officials are making little effort to defend the legality of the sanctions. Instead, they have begun to send direct and indirect messages to Tokyo that something much more important than auto parts is at stake.
>
> Japanese leaders, they now argue, have an essential decision to make: whether it is worth winning points in front of the World Trade Organization if the long-term cost is harm to their overall relationship with the United States.

Japan had broad based world-support and, as far as they were concerned, the U.S. was ready to hang itself. The U.S., from the Japanese perspective, fell totally and completely into their trap.

Japan, as expressed by the news article, won backing at the World Trade Organization against U.S. actions. The U.S. was getting a black eye and there was no escape.

Reuters on May 29, 1995 reported:

> Trade sources said envoys from Australia, India and Indonesia also condemned ``unilateral actions'' – a reference to the U.S. imposition of 100 per cent tariffs on Japanese luxury cars to go into full effect on June 28.
>
> An ambassador from one key emerging country told Reuters Washington's move was a challenge to the structure for solving disputes created under the WTO with U.S. support. ``They are holding the whole system hostage,'' he added.

On ABC's *This Week with David Brinkley*, "... Democratic Sen. Bill Bradley of New Jersey and former Trade Representative Carla Hills, warned that America could get hurt by playing hardball with Japan."

Last minute intense negotiations were taking place in Geneva. As negotiations approached the June 28th deadline, Japan opened personal attacks against U.S. lead negotiator, Mickey Kantor.

Japan's chief negotiator, Ryutaro Hashimoto, was someone who was an open foe of the United States. He, as chairman of the Japan War Bereaved Families Association, fiercely opposed apologies for Japan's wartime actions. He represented Japan in U.S. trade negotiations. He gave up nothing.

Moreover, ever since his childhood friend, Nakusan Kaitu, was uncovered as a U.S. operative, Hashimoto was more committed than ever to pay back the U.S. since much of what Nakusan learned and transmitted to U.S. authorities came from Hashimoto, his lifetime friend. The Japanese trade negotiator blamed, with his heart and soul, the U.S. for turning his friend against his own people.

So when Kantor presented Hashimoto with a kendo bamboo marital arts sword as a gift, Hashimoto, according to the news reports, "brandished the sword, known as a shinai, under Kantor's nose with a broad smile, he then handed it to an aide...."

If this wasn't insult enough for Kantor and the U.S., Hashimoto told the world media that "...arguing with Kantor is 'more scary than even my wife when I come home drunk.'" This was a supreme insult to Kantor.

On Sunday, June 25th I got a call from someone at the State Department. He said he got my name and number from former President Bush who suggested that he call me to ask: "What do I think it will take for the Japanese to throw in the towel?"

Just the type of question I like getting on a Sunday morning. The fellow's name was Talbor or something like that, and he had that attitude which suggested to me that he hadn't any idea of why he was calling me and, better said, who I was since I surmise I didn't show on State's computers.

My answer didn't much impress him either. I told him to tell ex-President Bush that I did not think they would cave in; I could not think of anything to scare them off except telling them that the U.S. was going to covertly support military action against them by one of the many Asian countries that hated the Japanese. I said I was sorry but that's all that came to mind. Personally, I didn't think any threat would stop them.

It was a good thing, however, before hanging up with Talbor that I asked him how much longer Kantor was going to hang around getting himself and the U.S. insulted.

Talbor said that meetings were scheduled until and including the deadline date of June 28th. Then, if no agreement, Clinton would have to make the hard decisions.

I thought for a brief moment and said. "I don't think Hoshimoto will be there Wednesday if you don't reach any agreement by then."

"What do you mean?" he asked sharply.

"The Japanese are figuring we are desperate as per your calling me. Hoshimoto, I predict, may fall ill Monday or Tuesday and will leave suddenly for Japan eviscerating final meetings and any tactical ploys you may have in mind."

"I'm not sure," I quickly added. "But it is a tactic of theirs that they use in critical situations. Quite frankly I'm surprised they haven't used it already."

"Thanks," Talbor said and hung up.

On June 28th, the U.S. won. I'm sorry, I don't know how. I only know that Kantor burst into Hoshimoto's room unannounced at 8:45 AM, hours before the scheduled meeting. According to Kantor's historical remark to the press: "*He (Hoshimoto) was very pragmatic. He understood the choices we faced and that was the turning point.*"

With those words and on that day, the U.S. became the supreme and sole world superpower.

It is also the day history will ultimately record that David Rockefeller and his elitist centrix came in control of the world, because it allowed them to move to control leaderships in all major world countries and financial centers, and the day America's future as a true democracy was seriously compromised.

David Rockefeller called his friend George Bush, now living a comfortable life in retirement, with two sons in politics, one currently the Governor of Texas: "I told you they would pay, George. And I'm not finished with them yet!"

CHAPTER 13
THE ADVERTISEMENT

I f one didn't believe the Japanese, or one wasn't clear about the true U.S. agenda, it became crystal clear in 1996, when President Bill Clinton violated all historical precedent and went to Israel to campaign for Shimon Peres.

In 1992, toward the end of George Bush's term, the U.S. made a deal with Shimon Peres.

Peres had a very large ego, and he couldn't stand losing numerous times in succession in his bid for high office in the State of Israel. He wanted to get the last laugh in his battle with critics and thus he was ripe for a deal with the United States. The U.S. would support him, with all its power, but he, like Boris Yeltsin, in Russia would become a puppet of the U.S. agenda.

However, despite all the U.S. help, he couldn't wrestle away in 1992 the nomination in his own party from Yitzhak Rabin, who ultimately won the national elections and became Prime Minister.

The U.S. made the best of it, when Peres moved into the number two slot in government. Through the years, with U.S. tactics and strategies, he got Rabin to come around to much of his (the U.S.'s) perspective.

While Rabin and Peres seemingly became close, both men never forgot the times they openly fought and detested one another, and they had different visions regarding what Israel should forego in the name of peace. Thus, Rabin, without knowing it, put himself in the same situation as Gorbachev, in the former Soviet Union. He shared the same fate.

Yitzhak Rabin, in the fall of 1995, right after the U.S. victory over Japan, was assassinated . The net result is that control over the Mid East peace process fell into the hands of Shimon Peres.

The *Dow Jones News Service* wrote about the arrested assassin of Yitzhak Rabin: "On Sunday, Yigal Amir said he carried secrets that 'will destroy everything. Everything until now was a mask' the 25 year old student said. The truth about the slaying, he said would 'turn the country upside down.'"

No one knew what Amir was talking about, but I certainly had strong suspicions that he wasn't far off from being in Oswald's shoes. However, since the time of Oswald, the power and people behind political assassinations have become quite sophisticated. What happens is that an entire situation with multiple buffers is set up, and usually all the buffers, who are links, are taken out, so that no matter if the shooter gets caught, there is no proof, no evidence, and it turns into a tall tale that a desperate assassin is left with to haunt him the rest of his life.

Look at the Kennedy Assassination. In the name of national interests they couldn't go anywhere with a real investigation unless word got out that they were investigating the President of the United States (Johnson), the FBI Director (Hoover), who Johnson appointed to that post for life, and Jackie Kennedy, the widow of the assassinated President.

Johnson would have had anyone on the Warren Commission pursuing such an avenue on a serious basis, put away, if not marked for death. Moreover, who was on the Warren Commission, none other that Allen Dulles the CIA Chief whom Kennedy fired regarding the Bay of Pigs fiasco and who carried no lost love for the slain President. No doubt, knowing how Dulles operated, that he pointed to organized crime and Jackie Kennedy. That sealed the report right there.

Nevertheless, after what is happening now in Israel and other countries throughout the world, in the name of "peace," and "international cooperation," warrants American citizens now knowing what happened in 1963. I don't want government to treat Americans as sheep, unaware of the true course being set by government for their futures.

When Italy elected a neo-fascist leader on March 28, 1994, out of alignment with the U.S. agenda, he soon fell. When John Majors, a critical ally to the U.S. agenda swooned in popularity, the opposition leader John Smith, died of a surprise heart attack at the age of 55. Tony Blair, who decreed himself a Clinton clone, replaced him. Regardless of who wins, in the future, in the Spring 1997 British elections, whether Majors or Blair, either way, a representative of the new world agenda continues in power.

The primary election of concern in the Spring of 1996 was Israel. This small country was critical since the future had an important nexus to what resolved itself in the Mid-East.

The dynamic of Rabin's assassination is best expressed through the death of another Israeli, a young soldier named Nahshon Waxman.

In October 1994, he was captured and held hostage by the Muslim terrorist group, Hamas. This was on the eve of when Nobel peace prizes were going to be jointly awarded in Stockholm to Arafat, Rabin and Peres. The entire dynamic for U.S. sponsored peace was in effect and now there could be no open relationship between the key parties until soldier Waxman's fate was resolved.

While the U.S., Israel and Arafat, quickly pushed every door, none opened. After I analyzed world markets with my machine intelligent computer systems, I was telling my friends and clients that the Waxman hostage situation was going to be resolved quickly.

Several days later, troops were haphazardly sent to supposedly save Waxman from the terrorists holding him hostage. Not only did Waxman die, but so did others, including fellow Israeli soldiers.

On October 14, 1994, I specifically wrote as follows:

> "By now, we hope we have prompted your analytical thinking to realize that this kid was totally sacrificed for the Mid East peace plan agenda. The U.S. knew that as long as he was held for political ransom that the Mid East peace talks were stalled at an important juncture. This had to be eliminated as an issue and thus the U.S. itself probably accessed its deepest operatives to locate him for the raid where everyone knew he would not emerge alive. However, they achieved their goal of neutralizing the issue and thus again the government proved to itself that its ends justify whatever means to accomplish them."

I never had any respect for Shimon Peres. However, now I lost respect for Rabin for standing by, knowing that it was unlikely Waxman would be recaptured alive. Moreover, he put prime Israeli troops into unnecessary jeopardy, some of whom also lost their lives.

Ironically, now with Rabin himself out of the way as an impediment to the Mid-East peace process, it could continue on, in parallel to Waxman's removal.

Peres had already pledged to do whatever he was told to do. Now, only one thing remained. He had to get elected Prime Minister. However, remember that Peres is a loser. So to the dismay of the "family of nations," Peres screwed everything up.

First, Peres called for quick elections. In one of the supreme ironies of life, his popularity was riding high because of the Rabin assassination. Peres waited his entire life for public acceptance and popularity. Now, since he had it on the back of the assassination of "his friend" Yitzhack Rabin, he couldn't wait to get elected and called for early elections in May, 1996.

Second, Hamas, after Peres put his foot immediately into his mouth, committed a number of serious suicide bombings, and as a result Peres' popularity disappeared as quickly as it arose.

Third, the U.S. had a lot at stake in the Mid East peace process. It needed Peres, who was the Boris Yeltsin of Israel. Thus, they had to call off the elections or do something else drastic to help their man, Peres.

So for the first time in history, a sitting U.S. President went to Israel, a foreign State, to stump for a political candidate. This was beyond the pale, as far as I was concerned.

I prepared the following advertisement that went on the back page of the *Jerusalem Post* on May 17, 1996, and it nearly took up the entire back page, a page equal in size to the Wall Street Journal's page:

Don't vote for Peres

An American company pleads with you not to vote for Shimon Peres.

By: Noah Guerin

**If you vote Peres officially into office, you will
cause the greatest disrespect not only to Yitzhak
Rabin but to yourself and your ancestors. Let me
explain.**

In August 1991, at the time of the Russian coup, which
effectively removed Gorbachev from power, I
announced to my world wide clientele that Gorbachev
would be replaced by a leader who would comply with
G-7 interests: Boris Yeltsin. Gorbachev survived the
coup thanks to Ronald Reagan, who, was sensitive to
the risk and role Gorbachev assumed in the historical
break up of the Soviet Union. Take careful notice of
how Gorbachev, while still alive (*Time Magazine's Man of
the Century*), nearly never is interviewed by major U.S.
media about anything going on in the world today.

Others in the way of G-7 interests routinely do not
share Gorbachev's "good fortune" of living. These
include two Israelis: Nahshon Waxman and Yitzhak
Rabin. Cpl. Waxman was captured when the Nobel
Peace Prize was being awarded to Rabin, Arafat and
Peres. With the Mid East peace discussions at a critical
stage, those discussions were suspended pending
resolution of the Waxman hostage situation. Cpl.
Waxman thus was doomed to a quick resolution of his
situation and in fact did die during a hasty "rescue
mission," launched days after his capture. Once he was
out of the way, the "peace talks" could resume.

Peres, the Boris Yeltsin of Israel, was and still is the
favorite of the Mid East deal makers. Despite support
of G-7, Peres never received the vote but assumed a
critical role as Foreign Minister. While Rabin, after his
election, bent to G-7 wishes, giving up much of the
West Bank, he, like Gorbachev, was reluctant to
cooperate fully; Gorbachev on Communism and
other matters and Rabin on Jerusalem and other

matters. Mr. Peres himself thus surely knows how *coincidental* and convenient Rabin's death is to the finalization of the global agenda for Mid East peace. **It is critical to those interests that Mr. Peres wins the election, now that Yitzhak Rabin, like Cpl. Waxman and Mikhail Gorbachev, is out of the way.**

Clinton came to Israel in mid-March not for Rabin, but to rehabilitate Peres after the Islamic suicide bombings. Peres at that time had no chance of winning the May elections he hastily called, seeing himself a shoe-in under the throes of the death of Rabin. With the suicide bombings, Peres' popularity plummeted to original low levels even faster than it soared under Rabin's assassination; the elections had to be canceled or something dramatic had to be done for Peres. Clinton thus came and restored Peres.

The visits to Israel by Clinton and G-7 and Arab leaders gave Israel global recognition. All this attention felt good, didn't it? However, you were deftly manipulated under the greater agenda where Israeli sovereign interests are not dominant or paramount. Do you genuinely believe that Israel's sovereign interests come first on anyone's list?

When Rabin was buried after his assassination, it looked like a "Mafia funeral" with all those "benefiting" from his death in attendance. Shimon Peres now seeks to capture the victory Rabin denied him. Israeli citizens must continue to vote for leadership which has no conflict of interest with Israeli sovereign interests. Think carefully about Yitzhak Rabin, Nahshon Waxman and Mikhail Gorbachev when you cast your vote. Consider carefully claims from Shimon Peres that he is carrying out the Rabin peace agenda. Rabin didn't like Peres, we don't, and considering that Peres failed to win in elections four times, you shouldn't like Peres either.

You are free to copy, reprint or distribute this advertisement in its entirety. It will be our only ad. We felt compelled to speak on this disturbing issue. While the above constitutes matters of opinion, it speaks for the need of Israeli citizens to vote for leaders solely dedicated to Israeli sovereign interests, and who are not puppets of outside forces. Outside powers have perhaps a transient interest in the fate and future of Israel, but have a direct and permanent interest in gaining control over Jerusalem. Without Jerusalem, Israeli citizens may as well pack up and move, as once discussed, to Uganda.

After the elections, which Peres lost by some 20,000 votes, it was revealed Peres made unconscionable secret deals impacting his country and its citizens. No one knew about them, and he wasn't going to reveal them *until after he won.*

Ruth Wisse, a professor at Harvard University, astutely wrote, in part, after Peres lost, as follows in op-ed section of the *Wall Street Journal.* She was manifestly upset at the way the media was acting during and after the Israeli elections.

"That a change in Israeli leadership, the most normal and necessary procedure of democracy, should occasion this kind of fear- and hate-mongering is proof of danger indeed– only not where the media pretend to find it."

{M}ost of the American media have joined the cheerleading squad of the imagined "New Middle East." More like fundamentalist believers than investigative reporters, journalists have been parroting the peace rhetoric rather than tapping into the public's concern over the Oslo arrangements. And when the truth of Israeli feelings was expressed in an election, the press turned on that expression as if it were a personal betrayal of all that is good and decent.

...Since they were not consulted in the first place over the Oslo accords, this vote represented their first referendum on its merits. If 56% of Israel's Jews and a majority of its electorate voted against Mr. Peres and for Mr. Netanyahu, it was because they had thoughtfully (and in many cases regretfully) concluded that the agreements had worsened their situation and hence had to be revised. Far from being a vote for fear, the election is more obviously a vote against fear and for common sense and confidence in Israel's robust future."

When Boris Yeltsin ran in Russia's first elections, later in the year, the U.S. did not make the same mistakes it made in Israel. Clinton kept his mouth shut. However, after Yeltsin's victory, *ABC's Nightline* on several occasions interviewed U.S. media masters behind the Yeltsin victory. They admitted not only doing critical focus group studies; his advertising, telling him what to say and how to act, staging songfests, directing him to disco dance, arranging rallies, *but also paying off journalists to get Yeltsin lots of favorable press and his opponents literally none.*

Why were there no voices in government shouting opposition as to what was going on?

Finally, there was one.

CHAPTER 14
NIKKO, MEET CHRISTINE

Newt Gingrich, Speaker of the House of Representatives, on *Meet the Press* criticized U.S. efforts to control foreign leadership.

Here's what he said:

> MR. RUSSERT: Did President Clinton make a mistake with his tacit support of Shimon Peres in the Israeli election?

> REP. GINGRICH: Oh, I think so. I think, we, the   American people, have a good relationship with the people   of Israel, and the government the American people chooses should have a good relationship with the government the people of Israel choose. I think the same–there's a similar danger in Russia. . . . You know, we don't have a candidate in the Russian election. We shouldn't have a candidate in the Russian election.

> MR. RUSSERT: But President Clinton has been very   supportive of Boris Yeltsin.

> REP. GINGRICH:...**And it's very dangerous in the long run. The American nation cannot reach across the planet and pick the leadership of other countries.** Doesn't mean we shouldn't try to encourage movement towards democracy and free enterprise and private property and the rule of law, but when you personalize it–and in the first place, people are very fragile, and in the second place, they don't always do the same thing after the election they promised before the election.

> ....So building your foreign policy around a series of   personalities is ultimately very dangerous, and you lead people around the world to say, I mean, `Who are the   Americans to come in and tell us who we ought to elect?' And I think, frankly–and I'm not sure that Prime Minister Peres, who is a fine person and a tremendous leader, was particularly helped by the heavy hand of an American endorsement just before the election. I mean, it seemed to me that that doesn't necessarily say that the average Israeli–`This is the guy who's going to lead me, this is the guy who's going to side with Bill Clinton.' I just think it's very tricky when presidents get too directly involved in other countries' relationships.

I, for a few moments, was ecstatic hearing him say it. But he too was a lonely voice, and then I recalled George Bush's statement to me that winning battles is meaningless unless you win the war.

Bush told me the new world order agenda was in place and no one could change it. So with deep sorrow, I kept an eye open for attacks against the Speaker. They came and they continue.

I also received information that after the new Prime Minister, Binyamin Netanyahu, assumed office in Israel, that he was secretly visited by Henry Kissinger and Conrad Black. While you no doubt know Henry Kissinger, number one public Jewish ally to the Rockefellers, you might not know Conrad Black. He is among the handful of families that control the media; owning hundreds of newspapers world-wide including the *Jerusalem Post*, the only newspaper in Israel that supported the new Prime Minister.

The process of roping in the new Prime Minster had already commenced with the visit of these two individuals. How could I doubt the interpretation of the one who thought he was the President of the United States – as I will soon explain.

When I next saw Christine, I also knew that my time had come.

What surprised me was that they used Christine again. I was disappointed because, no matter how much I may have impressed them, they, for some reason, didn't think me smart enough to make the connection. I guess if they thought me smart, they would have figured I would be smart enough to join them, the winning team, and enjoy a rich and rewarding life.

Thus, one evening, twenty three years after I first met her, I saw Christine at Du Midi, a New York French restaurant I often ate at before taking in the theater.

I was with other people and as we were having our dessert, she walked in the door. She was by herself. We saw one another, embraced, and went through the "it's a small world routine." However, I knew that, as before, she was there for me.

She said why not have dinner together for old times sake the next evening, and she gave me the information on a little known restaurant I heard about off Hudson Street in Soho. It was a relatively new and informal fish restaurant owned by some of the people working at the Fulton fish market.

I told her I would love to, rejoined my friends, and sat there looking at a woman who didn't appear an iota less attractive after so many years. Strong memories hold themselves firm through time.

Her looking at me, with those beautiful eyes, was intended to forge into my mind who I was having dinner with the next evening. She no doubt knew I would be thinking about whether dinner would end in similar fashion to Acapulco 1973.

I figured that odds were 80% or more that she was there to hurt me. How badly I didn't know. But I would no doubt find out and I spent the next day preparing for the meeting by shopping the entire next morning around Chinatown and then preparing for my dinner with Christine.

Nikko was totally knowledgeable in the use of poison. She knew how to prepare not one but every variety of poison imaginable. Some would take effect in a second, some over several hours, some over several days and some even longer. And some had antidotes, and some did not.

This knowledge of poison was something carried on in her family through generations. Poison was used without question or remorse for aggressive and protective reasons. Without doubt, to my mind, this was the answer to President Bush's behavior after his return from Tokyo.

I prepared a concoction that would take effect two hours after ingestion, take two days to fully take hold, and which needed an antidote within two days thereafter.

I prepared the antidote and went to the Columbia University Library and in the stacks, two floors below ground level, hid the antidote behind a book, in a row of books, which seemingly hadn't been touched for years.

I then took the poison with me to my meeting with Christine. We were seated at a table set for four and I immediately slipped one of the empty wine glasses beneath the table. I spilled some of the poison into the glass and returned it to the table.

The wine came, and I tasted it, and approved it. I told the wine steward that I would pour the wine and rather than reach over for Christine's glass, I took the glass where the clear, transparent, poison had already dried onto the inside. I poured the wine for Christine and handed it to her. I asked the wine steward to remove the two other wine glasses and place settings.

The first glass and first sips are the only ones you can count on. It proved successful, especially when Christine herself had no real reason to realize that I would act so early on.

I wasn't of course sure what her instructions were. But that didn't matter. I assumed that she was there to hurt me and it wasn't long into our appetizer that I told her so.

She had told me that she still never married and that she could never find happiness with anyone. She was in advertising, and was in New York to do work with Young & Rubican. She said she might find herself having to stay in New York for three months.

I knew the scenario for sure. She was going to warm up the relationship tonight and then over the next three months during a night of bliss or during some set up, I would be compromised or hit.

I knew it wouldn't be long until she felt I was on to her because keeping my feelings hidden wasn't something I was expert at, and something I didn't want to become expert at.

So I got to the point.

"Christine. I am sorry to tell you this, but I poisoned you."

She paused as though she thought I was starting some kind of joke, and gave a little laugh.

" I am serious. It is a poison which will not do you serious harm for several days. I have the antidote. Unless you answer my questions and do what I say you will not get the antidote.

"And don't run out now and ask your friends for help. By the time they figure out the poison, it will be too late for you."

"What happened to you Noah? Have you gone mad?"

"Yes Christine, I'm mad. I'm really angry. Don't you think that I figured out our little tryst in Acapulco was something started by you? My ego wasn't big enough for me not to figure it out. If you want to play the role, go ahead and do it, but you are dying and I'm not kidding. You are wasting time and the type of questions I am going to ask you will not compromise you with those who sent you here for me."

"Noah........," she said, my catching her off guard so massively by telling her I poisoned her and that I knew all along she was no mere item of chance.

"Christine, I want a meeting with David Rockefeller himself: the big cheese. Before you think I'm crazy, I have little doubt at your persuasiveness when your life hangs in the balance. I will be in the main reading room of the New York Public Library at 10:30 AM tomorrow morning. Tell him I want him there and I will not tolerate any excuse for his not being there. No out of town. No, I don't know what you are talking about. Otherwise, you are dead and tell them that I will move to hunt him down as I no doubt expect that they will do the same with me."

I almost thought Christine was going to tell me that there was no way he would ever show up himself. However, she continued with her training.

"I don't know David Rockefeller. What has David Rockefeller have to do with me! I'm going to call the police right now."

"Be my guest. When you come back, I won't be here or anywhere to be found. But you're not going to call the police, are you Christine?

"Sure, if you want to be a hero you can achieve your mission by calling the police and having me arrested for doing what I have done and you will have damaged me as your friends sent you to do, no doubt. But you will be dead and I will deny it and when my attorneys dig into your background they are going to find a hundred men who probably would have reason to poison you. Can I help it if one of them succeeded?

"What are you going to tell them?" I continued. "That we are lovers? I'll be laughing with them."

This wild set of multi-dimensional arguments proved to be a strain on Christine. She didn't feel anything yet, so she surely thought I might be joking or putting one on her. Her training told her to stay cool.

"Let's have dinner then," she said "and we can talk about your little sick stunt."

If she was sent to New York to kill me, she wasn't going to have any conscience or remorse in doing it now.

"That's OK with me Christine," I said. "By the time we are finished with dessert, you are going to start feeling it. You will then have about two more hours to get back to the Hilton and make the necessary calls and contacts. Present your arguments quickly because by the middle of the night you are going to lose partial control of your autonomic system."

We sat there simply eating without saying anything because I knew she was praying that I was joking. She knew me well enough to know that if she felt the poison take effect that I wasn't joking about the rest, particularly because she knew what she had been sent to New York to do.

She never understood why her agency used her for me. She never understood the interest and she never understood why she had to do what she was sent to do. She couldn't ask questions.

Once she realized the poison was taking effect, and that her life was in my hands, she wasn't, with a husband, two sons and a daughter, ready to give up her life without seeing if they were going to honor my request.

Christine was married when she was with me in Acapulco. Not to my great surprise, her husband was a supervisor at the DIA (Defense Intelligence Agency). The agency first discouraged the marriage because Christine was too valuable a resource. However, when her husband agreed to close his eyes, to what she had to continue doing to operate for the agency, it received the blessings of the agency. I think this was what was bothering Christine when I was with her in Acapulco in 1973. It's hard to accept a husband knowingly closing his eyes to what she had to routinely do.

She wasn't anxious to tell me too much more because, among other reasons, she wanted to get going to see if this obtuse request I made was going to be honored. If she didn't think there was a chance of her coming out of it, she might have killed me right there in the restaurant for spite.

But when I tried to ask her more, she showed her underlying toughness by telling me with controlled anger: "Do you want me to set up this meeting or do you want to play twenty questions with me?"

CHAPTER 15
THE LION AND THE FLY

I stayed at the St. James hotel on West 45th Street that evening, paying cash.

The next day, I was at the Main 42nd Street New York Public Library at 10:15 AM. I was seated in the main reading room. At 10:30 AM sharp a husky fellow walked in pushing a wheel chair. In the wheel chair was Christine, who obviously no longer had the slightest doubt about being poisoned. She could no longer walk among other new limitations for someone like her.

The big fellow simply wheeled Christine over to me. I didn't know, for sure, whether they were going to do anything there, but I thought not. I bet my life on that thought, by the way.

The big fellow said:" Mr. Rockefeller is in the limousine outside. He'll speak to you there...Tell me where we can find the antidote."

You have to keep to your agenda. "I want to speak to him here."

"Mr. Rockefeller will not come into the library."

"Have a good day then."

I could read the big fellow's face. He wanted to join the line behind Christine in teaching me and my big mouth a lesson. I had already caused problems for those who were accustomed to quickly disposing of them.

He picked up his cellular phone and said something.

They stood there staring at me the entire ten minutes. Christine really now hated me. Why? For saving my life? For standing up against them? Or was it because I used her to save myself?

Ten minutes later the big cheese came in. Like a lot of powerful men, he was of small posture, and offset it by ruling everything around him. Napoleon paled in power next to David Rockefeller.

He wouldn't at first sit down. He stood next to me looking down at me like a master over a dog who bit his child, and told me that he wouldn't talk there.

I said. "Mr. Rockefeller sit down. You probably have had this entire place probed during the evening and probably everyone around me is one of yours. You can have Bruno over there search me for any electronic devices and if you prefer I can take off my clothes here but that will only bring us more attention."

David Rockefeller was trying to figure out if I knew that his people had checked out the entire library throughout the evening for anything and everything including my hiding the antidote there. They were clever enough to know that I wouldn't be carrying it. He also wondered if I knew they thoroughly searched my apartment and contacted Nikko as a source for the poisons used. However, while Nikko told them what she had taught me, she couldn't tell which variation I used and Christine was someone David Rockefeller, for reasons then unknown to me, wanted to save.

David Rockefeller sat down and said to me: "Tell Christine where she can find the antidote."

Rockefeller liked giving orders. If I simply told them where they could find the antidote, they would have all stood up and left.

"It's at the Columbia University Main Library. It is behind a book. Call me on my cellular number when you get there, and I'll give you the Dewey Decimal number for it."

"Bruno" wheeled Christine out, and, when Rockefeller remained seated, I had little doubt that there were Rockefeller people all over the reading room.

Rockefeller then surprised me by getting right to the point.

"You cannot take out ads like the one you took out against Peres. You caused U.S. interests much damage and with your having spoken to so many Presidents...is dangerous to the interests of the country."

He was speaking as though he were President of the United States. How silly of me. He was the real U.S. monarch. "I'm a regular U.S. citizen. I spoke to them as such. And there is no reason to do away with me for upsetting not U.S. interests, but your interests and plans for your new world order."

"Who do you think you are, speaking to me like that? I should have gotten rid of you a long time ago, you little maggot. Don't you realize that you are trying to undermine agendas in place by the finest minds in this country, all of whom are just as good and loyal Americans as you?"

"I know your little game too well," I countered. "You have all these elitist groups and they have everyone powerful and influential in them.

"There's a whole group legitimately fearful of a nuclear holocaust and you have been their savior. There's another group looking for global capitalism and riches from Russia to South America. You have been a deliverer to them. There's another group that is seriously concerned about world pollution: you are the gateway to a cleaner and safer world to them. There is another group that strictly wants to see the U.S. as the sole superpower in the world: you have provided it to them.

"Everyone looks at you from a different window and sees you just as you want them to see you. You are a saint to their eyes and minds and they can't see the forest from the trees. You have been trying to snap me up for years, to get me into your grasp, and you have failed, because I don't operate on the same batteries as mostly everyone else you can control.

"And if you didn't fear the truth you wouldn't need to control me or kill me and you wouldn't need to play the country for fools.

"I know your real agenda. I knew right away that you spit on America for failing to give Nelson a Presidential opportunity. I knew that you wanted from the first to have one central world government, with Rockefellers behind it, so you could protect your world wide investments just as Nakusan Kaitu thought I could help him and his family protect theirs."

Rockefeller was impressed and calmly responded: "This country was built on immigrants from different parts of the world. I have a simple question for you. At any point of time, could any honest working person from any part of the world come here to America to give himself a better future and make himself a citizen?"

"I thought," I said in response, "that a person had to be in flight from persecution to seek sanctuary within our borders."

Rockefeller gave me an askance look: "They are flowing in every day from Mexico, from Canada, by boat, ship, helicopter, sea plane...everyone wants to come here.... So instead of everyone coming here to seek the opportunities they all want, the new era will extend the opportunities they seek to everyone on the planet. Capitalism will bring peace. Strong, unified government will bring protection from nuclear warfare and nuclear proliferation. America will have won. We are in control. Peace and democracy are being carried everywhere."

"That's why Rabin got shot? That's why we did everything to fix the Israeli elections for Peres? That's why we did everything to make sure Yeltsin won?"

"Look," Rockefeller tried in a last desperate attempt to carry me over to his side. "You can't have the people making mistakes with dangerous candidates. That's how Hitler came into power. People are always going to be taken in by extremism, especially if they have to undergo some difficult times.

"Nationalism, like religion, has been the basis for many wars. I know your ad showed you are willing to fight for Jerusalem; for your people, but that kind of attitude has resulted in many wars, many deaths."

I said: "That kind of argument from someone like you has come to control many key American minds. However, look how it has had to be done: you control the media, you control government policy, you restrict key nominations to individuals who are part of your agenda, or you set them up to come over to you; you fix foreign candidates and elections; you intervene in foreign affairs and elections; you define the scope of democracy; you conclude that Americans are inept to make good judgments; you have appointed yourself and your band as saviors....as hidden secret monarchs."

Rockefeller replied: "We have been successful. Aren't we the sole superpower? Isn't the world at a better state and stage of peace than ever before? Haven't we spread democracy and capitalism to the world? Haven't we provided the world with more opportunity? Aren't we doing away with oppressive governments who use torture and other coercive ways? Haven't we given the world better health and provided assistance to millions throughout the world. I don't understand what you are bitching about unless you want the world to regress to where it used to be in its violent past."

"Look at the stock market soaring," I countered. "Look at interest rates. Look at the lies and deceptions told the American public concerning unemployment and the true reasons the market is soaring and why interest rates are staying at low levels. How long do you think we will be able to sustain it?"

"A long time," Rockefeller said. "We have just opened up the rest of the world to capitalism and democracy and we have won. America and American companies will dominate, just as the Japanese wanted to dominate. That's the reason I'm here. You were right about the Japanese, and George Bush and myself were taken in by misleading actions and statements from people we thought were reliable friends in Japan. So we wanted you and I'm here because you were right and we were wrong about Japan. But you are wrong, even about your dear Israel and Jerusalem. You are going to lose it."

He could see that he was upsetting me. "Don't you understand that we were set up for peace. Yes, Peres is a loathsome figure. We have to use abominable people to do our work. Yeltsin was even worse than Peres and look how far he has come. We know you can't stand people who double deal their own country; but they are going to be heroes there and Peres would have been a hero there, if he brought peace and stability... and he might have done so if you didn't put in your two cents."

"Come on," I said. My one little ad didn't change the election. It was in hands far greater than even yours.

Rockefeller countered: "Won't you admit that more wars and deaths have resulted from religion than almost anything else you could think of. Even persecution of Jews stem from religion. We are creating a world of tolerance. Jews are everywhere."

"Except in the synagogue."

"Are you a religious fanatic!" Rockefeller exclaimed. "Would you see more deaths based on religious arguments?"

"There are different approaches," I said. "Jerusalem has been in the hands of many different nations throughout time. *Perhaps if one nation would have simply taken the time to understand that Jerusalem belongs to God not man that it would have served as the foundation for peace among nations.* Perhaps we need the qualities of self-sacrifice and generosity and respect to see the real answers."

"Don't be naive. We have made more progress than anyone before us," declared Rockefeller, seemingly as the world leader he was. "Your suppositions are not based on deep study. Mine are based on the best studies and minds in the world. Why do you persist?"

"Because your end results in world homogeneity. One world. No religion, except capitalism. No nations. No diversity. McDonalds and franchises throughout the world. Perhaps even one language. One government. Did you ask the citizens of the world whether they want to go in this direction?"

"Do you think they know where they want to go? Do you want to leave it to chance whether we avoid nuclear holocaust or don't you realize we must take control of everything to guarantee safety not only for us but the entire world?"

"And you are in the center of it."

"Someone has to be in the center," Rockefeller countered. "While you have a long list of complaints, you cannot deny the achievements."

"The complaints outweigh the achievements. *We were founded as a Nation with a Constitution and everything you are doing belittles what Americans fought for and against. Your interventions and your self-righteous proclamations that you have achieved good is in line with a benevolent monarchy not a true democracy.* We can achieve similar results without your using the technique of any means justifying Rockefeller declared beneficial ends."

"You know I have been patient with you. I want to reach an understanding that our meeting never took place."

"Why because the truth will ruin your design?"

"Yes."

"So that means the truth is your enemy."

Rockefeller paused. "And yours."

Rockefeller then softened his threat: "Noah, we want you with us. You can achieve more by joining us than by being so stubborn and resisting us. You may be wrong. You might find that we are what the people really do want. Won't you at least consider it?"

I could only focus on his threat: "Look you have the power to do me in by surprise and at will whenever you want to. But don't miss as I am sure you won't. But I want to think that even someone like yourself, whom I consider a world danger, will not sleep when he thinks he has to kill off someone like me, who simply opposes what he stands for. If I quote everything you said you will deny it and no doubt your army will put into place a barrage of critics and commentary to make people laugh at what I have to say.

"*However, somewhere you will slip.* I know you believe you are above it because the people are swallowing so much. But they are not fools. Something is going to happen which will galvanize Americans to see they are being mistreated. They already are getting the sense they are economic slaves. You control the entire Federal Reserve. You are claiming there is no inflation, while they see their savings evaporate; with college costs soaring through the roof, with car costs, health insurance costs, medical costs, rent, food, housing all requiring more and more money as America becomes poorer and poorer as a nation. You have masked it beautifully with the artificially low interest rates and the soaring stock market. You have created an Argentine market, which must keep on soaring lest the entire structure collapses, as one day it must and will. And little do Americans know that by that day you will have your new world order in place and you will be living in some newly established world capital which will be free of the conditions you will have left this country in. You will be joined by the new elite of America, and America will be the dump you intended it to be the day they let your brother Nelson down."

"You tell that crap to anyone and they will put you away."

"How about putting me away for why America hasn't solved the drug problem; it's educational problems. We have lotteries reaping billions of dollars while the educational structure disintegrates where children are entering college with junior high school skills. *The drug problem is expanding throughout the nation as millions of new children are protected from cigarettes while being moved to the more expensive criminal profits of drugs.* You can't tell me that you – the man who solved all that long laundry list of world problems– can't stop drugs in the United States. You want to stop it as much as General Motors wants car thieves to stop stealing cars. They have both become an essential part of the economy."

"You are delusional, and if you ever think you can stop us, we are going make you a public laughing stock. I just don't understand you Noah Guerin. There are few men, sane men I would add, who could turn down what I am offering you. You can do more from the inside I am telling you. We will send you business. You will have a staff to run your business, help you in your research. You will meet those invidious minds you detest and can make your points. If you don't accept you should really see someone professional for help. I'm sorry that's my honest opinion. I can't believe you can be sane and turn me down. I have to admit that I can't remember anyone who has ever done it before."

I saw that David Rockefeller would let me live because, if I denied his "generous" offer, he wanted to prove to me how insane I was in doing it. Incredibly, I must have earned further admiration for probably being the only person he would sit down in his life who would reject a golden goose offer.

However, I knew what I was doing, I couldn't be swayed, and I knew it was a function of time before Rockefeller would make a mistake, one which would forge the issues to Americans as to the lies and deceptions they have been subject to for so long. One which would open up the American consciousness to what is going on, and provide a platform to remove an improperly entrenched leadership, and reinstate a leadership which honors this Nation, and the principles and precepts upon which it was built.

CHAPTER 16
THE MISTAKE

After seeing the radar images of TWA Flight 800 on the CBS evening news on Wednesday, July 17, 1996, I didn't waste any time in getting in touch with my cousin, Robert Guerin. He lived in Westbury, Long Island and worked for Grumman Aircraft. As a long time employee of Grumman, he enjoyed the very type of networking I needed.

I had no doubt in my mind, after looking at the radar images, that it was a missile that took down TWA Flight 800.

I thought the government, now accustomed to institutionalized lying and deceit, might try to cover up the truth.

Those radar images were immediately confiscated by the FBI, who would not release them for public view. Brazenly and boldly, the government and the media referred to the radar images as nothing more than an "anomaly."

I, and every expert I know, have never seen an "anomaly" which shows on a radar screen six to eight seconds before an implosion and ceases with it!

What Robert Guerin could do as an employee of Grumman was contact some of the best military consultants in the country. He did call several of them, and immediately determined what the entire professional community believed, from their own network of people, that the Navy took down the plane with an "errant" unarmed missile.

The word was that it was a Stinger missile, which has a range of 24,000 feet, with an Aegis guidance system, and a capability of locking into the plane's transponder area.

The professional network was sure the missile wasn't armed. But they made it clear, that a collision into the transponder area would disable both the black boxes, the transponder, and radio communication simultaneously. If the crew still were trying to communicate, there would be no record of it. This network believes that the missile went through the aircraft, and is buried somewhere at sea.

Early newspaper reports confirmed this. The downing of the plane occurred on Wednesday July 17, 1996. The *Jerusalem Post* on July 21st reported from French intelligence sources that a Navy missile took down the aircraft. On July 22nd the *London Times* reported: "An American spy satellite positioned over the Brookhaven national laboratory on Long island is said to have yielded important information about the crash. A law enforcement official told the *New York Post* that the satellite pictures show an object racing up to the TWA jet, passing it, **then changing course** and smashing into it."

The leading local Long Island newspaper, *Newsday*, wrote as follows: "An early trail on a radar from Islip shows something rising, tracking toward the plane, circling to the front of the plane and then disappearing in the plane's underbelly, federal sources said."

While first evidences were strongly consistent with what I and a lot of other people knew, the government then pulled the plug on everything. The government determined that it didn't want the truth out, and everyone, including foreign powers and the foreign press, simply shut up, because the world's sole superpower had made its wishes known.

However, it seemed that Pierre Salinger wasn't made privy to the private wishes of the U.S. government. Salinger was a man who was a reliable and respected journalist for decades, former Press Secretary to John F. Kennedy, who had never misled the media and the public before.

When Pierre Salinger asserted that he had evidence that it was a missile, he was derided as an old man by the media, one who was taken in by material on the Internet, and FBI agents paid him a visit. Thereafter, total silence.

There is no shame in the degree of distrust which the government is willing to implant onto the entire nation, just to force their version of reality upon all Americans, young and old alike. On what basis does the

FBI keep interviews, photos, radar and satellite images secret from Americans? Do you think the cloak of national interests and secrets is being misused and Americans abused? The national interest would very well be served if *everything* was revealed. The damage of TWA Flight 800 is greater than the deaths of more than 230 people. It is evidence of serious damage to the nation via an abusive government.

One young woman told *Newsday*, that she not only had seen a missile from her parent's boat, but photographed it. The FBI confiscated her photos and negatives. She said that if she had not seen what she had, she would believe what she saw on television.

My cousin, Robert, called me on Friday, two days after the accident. He told me about a secretary to a top Grumman official, who believed she might have captured the downing of TWA Flight 800.

She lived in Carle Place, the town next to Robert's. I asked Robert to arrange for me and him to visit with her at her home.

When we got to her home, she was there with her husband, who was a CPA in the city, and her two children. She and her husband appeared quite nervous.

When you work for a major military contractor, you know not to make waves. There isn't any room at military contractors for whistle blowers of any kind, or for anyone who isn't smart enough not to open a can of worms against the U.S. government, without whom Grumman would cease to exist.

On July 17th, at the very time of the incident with TWA Flight 800, she was at a bridal shower in a seaside restaurant in the Hampton Bays. While many others were filming the party with their personal camcorders, she happened to be filming in the right direction.

She and her husband looked at the tape and there it was! A missile, in the far distance, moving towards the plane. They told us that the plane appeared to move away from the missile, but the missile changed direction and went into the plane, all in the matter of a second or two!

The wife already heard that the government was going to stonewall the entire incident. The couple concluded if they turned in the tape, they could harm Grumman's relationship with the government, and theirs with Grumman. They felt that whatever they did, this videotape was going to cause them grief. Their instincts were correct.

I asked them who knew about the tape. They said a lot of people at Grumman. I asked who knew what was on the tape. No one, yet, but us, they said. I told them to never reveal to anyone what was on their tape.

They engaged me as their attorney.

I told them that their instincts were right. The tape could cause them untold misery. But since they had already made the tape known, it was a matter of time before the FBI came knocking on their door.

I then told them what I knew they wanted to hear.

I told them to let me have the tape, and I would edit out the evidence of what really happened and edit back in alternative footage. No one would have reason to know anything, unless we or they specifically told anyone. I would make them and us a full copy of the original, in case we needed a full copy in the future.

It sounded good to them. They were in deep trouble, and I thought they knew they had to keep their mouths shut. Nevertheless, I reminded them again to never reveal what they had to anyone.

On Saturday, July 20th the government issued a formal plea, only three days after the incident, for any eyewitness, or anyone else having any evidence, to contact them.

Newsday even remarked that this was an unusual appeal. It was first proof that the government was out to identify anyone who could undermine their agenda, and to neutralize anything standing in its way.

I took the original of the tape, and, with Robert, went to my apartment in the city. I had a special recorder, which enabled me to quickly make two full duplicates of the video.

With sophisticated computer editing software, I proceeded to edit each frame of the evidence, in accord with what I told the couple who gave it to us.

It was more or less easy to take another section of the tape, where accidentally she recorded the floor, and put it in place of the evidence of the incident.

However, I also had the audio to deal with. I recorded the audio from the edited out section and moved it on top of the new edited segment. *Unless anyone had reason to know*, no one would know anything.

We returned to the couple, the edited original tape and one full duplicate of the complete original.

Days later, the couple was visited by the FBI and turned over the edited original tape. It was one of many videotapes picked up that day by the FBI. The FBI had confiscated all of her friends' videotapes too. No one got anything back.

Robert and I and the couple waited for many months for the truth to emerge from the government. However, the stonewall was in full force and effect, and it never did. We all couldn't believe it, and the couple's anxiety grew and grew. Some people just find it difficult to deal with stress.

CBS did two major pieces on TWA Flight 800; one on *60 Minutes* and the other on *48 Hours*. Instead of shouting that something smells in the government's position, they were selling the government line and otherwise standing silent to facts known to them. Were they under pressure that disclosure would undermine "national interests?" Wasn't anyone brave enough to stand up to government misuse of the "national interests," standard?

The importance of an independent media, discharging their fiduciary responsibilities as members of the fourth estate, to offset abuse of government power, is clearly seen via an *ABC's 20/20* piece on whether the government had advance warning of the Oklahoma City bombing. The media uncovered witnesses and film showing government agents searching for a bomb prior the explosion around the building. ATF agents were further told NOT to come to work that day. They simply never told anyone else in the building, including the day care center with all those children in it. You would think after the story aired that there would be a firestorm of interest. There was only silence.

I took great offense at President Clinton's political use of children after the Oklahoma City bombing. On April 28, 1995, I wrote as follows to clients, paralleling the position Bill Cosby took nearly two years later, when he lost his only son:

> A parent has two children. One dies in March 1995 due to a wanton shooting in his neighborhood. The second dies in April 1995 at the day care center at the Federal Building in Oklahoma. Is there anything more emotionally wrenching about the death of the second child than the first? Answer: absolutely not. The first and second deaths were as a result of depraved indifference to human life. Why should the President of the United States be so overly distraught over the death of the second child (representing 10-20 children) than the first (representing thousands of children each year). The only conclusion is that the President of the United States is reacting to an attack on the U.S. government and doesn't give a hoot over the first death as the second death. Further, it provided him with a platform to attack the right and thus the Republicans.

> You see the real item to be upset about emotionally is the indifference of the U.S. government to what is allowed on TV. Here is where the desensitization first takes place. That is why people can go about blowing up buildings with children in it and otherwise thousands upon thousands of children are murdered each year. How can a President of the United States be so upset nationally over the death of 10-20 children who died simultaneously over the deaths of thousands of similar children whose futures are snuffed out by depraved indifference actions in our everyday society. It is political and self-serving....

The most critical and persuasive thing to my mind, and one of the biggest mistakes, is when the government called what I saw, an "anomaly," to render it insignificant, while at the same time confiscating it from public view. Sadly, *60 Minutes* and *48 Hours*, while using the government characterization, failed to show it to the American public or comment on it, even though they had already broadcast it on the *CBS Evening News* immediately after the explosion. Anyone seeing it, as I did, would know it's not an anomaly, *and, as already emphasized by me, anomalies don't appear six to eight seconds before the implosion and then cease with it!!!*

The FBI openly and vociferously took the position that it has discounted no theory. All theories are in place including the missile theory, paying homage to the hundred plus eyewitnesses. However, while the FBI says this, the NTSB gets to do the dirty work by coming up with alternative theories, many lambasted because they expose Boeing and other large companies to liability. However, the main one, relied on by the NTSB, was a spark in the fuel tank, which took out the entire plane, by igniting pressurized fuel vapors.

This theory woke up the trial attorneys, who in unison said that it made a lot of sense.

Why did the government jump for joy?

If the attorneys could sell it to a jury or juries, and get one or more verdicts for the victims against the airline and other parties, it would be the American public, through the judicial process, which would conclude what really happened. Then the entire government would be off the hook by the deeds of the American public itself.

Why does the FBI still hold the missile theory open? If they cast it off and subscribed to any other theory and then one day some person, like me, knocks on the door of the media with a tape of the actual implosion, the country will lose trust and confidence in the FBI, and justly so. The new world order cannot jeopardize the integrity of the FBI. Thus, since they know what really happened, they can never say that it didn't.

Why are they going through all this trouble? It's a mistake they shouldn't have made because it opens the doors to so many other things. However, they have gotten away with everything. **That is the reason why Americans must clamor for truth, and a free press that acts as the catalyst for the clamor for truth. The obfuscation of truth regarding the Kennedy Assassination was the platform to where we are today. It is important to realize that my interpretation to President Nixon of what happened is not important. It could be true, close to true, or it could be wrong. What is true, however, is** that the American people were lied to and important secrets kept hidden under an umbrella of national interests, the non-disclosure of which has, in fact, undermined national interests.

On Sunday, October 20, 1996, I was in La Jolla, California, doing some consulting work for one of my law clients.

I was staying by his beach house on the Pacific Ocean, and I was out sitting close to the beach, when I saw an entourage of five joggers moving north along the beach.

William Jefferson Clinton was in California campaigning. Before heading for church, he was jogging with four secret service agents. He and his entourage stopped in front of me.

He knew who I was!

He introduced himself and admitted they knew I was out there. He asked if he could sit with me outside my client's beach house to talk.

I guess I am wired different from most other people. While others would find excitement about the President of the United States seeking them out for a conversation, I knew that this one couldn't be a good omen. I also didn't like him.

Why was I so biased against the President? What made me feel such an intense dislike for someone so many people seemed to warm up to. He certainly was personable. He was smooth as silk, and he made it sort of difficult for anyone not to like him.

However, Clinton was a spin master, like no other President we have ever had before. Clinton doesn't understand that when he squirms his way successfully out of a panoply of attacks, he sends a message to Americans, young and old alike, that if the President does it, they can't be faulted for doing it too.

So children put a spin on their stories to their teachers and parents, and adults put a spin on the way they do business. Clinton and this new moral ethic reflect the culmination of 40 years of disservice to the American people through the media's subliminal support of inappropriate messages and lifestyles.

Can subliminal messages of the media, and of Presidents, be inappropriate in an open democracy with freedom of speech? You tell me.

In the 50s and 60s, *Playboy Magazine* was a powerful force in American life for men. While many focused on the novel nude centerfolds, the damage was not via the pictures, but through the subliminal message to American men that many of their fellow male citizens were living great lives, with gorgeous women, riding around in glamorous cars. What about your life? Are you working 9-5 and coming home to the same home, wife, children, to yet another dreary evening? How about your weekends? Any excitement there? What about your fidelity to your wife? These guys, including your neighbor perhaps, are having a grand time with lots of different woman . Maybe not to the degree of Hugh Hefner, but a lot better than you. Are you going to settle for that dead, dreary, boring middle class American lifestyle with a loving wife and children? Is that all there is to your life?

It took until the 80s for the women of America to receive the Playboy message via the dual television series *Dallas* and *Dynasty*. What about your lives? What type of home do you live in? That guy you are cooking for: is he carrying his weight? Has he given you any gorgeous clothes or jewelry lately? Are you driving a Mercedes Benz? No! Couldn't you with a little luck have followed a different road and path, and lived the type of life these women are living – with the right fellow or two? Hey, it's not too late. Change you life. Your children, they don't give too much of a tinker for you, and anyhow it's the 80s. Aren't all the kids today from divorced homes?

The damage of the *Dallas* and *Dynasty* programs was also shown per the infamous J.R. Ewing who got most of America more excited about making $10 through a manipulation than by doing a honest hour of work.

The great life could be achieved by changing your goals. Morality, ethics, religion, family, all became secondary to career, physical and mental prowess, and manipulation and machination of others. Life became a game, with the winners counted per the size of their homes and the flamboyance of their lifestyles.

America had a J.R. Ewing, straight from the television scripts of *Dallas*, in the highest office of the land. Aside from the fact that President Clinton totally lied and misrepresented nearly every 1992 campaign promise made, highlighted by his pledge to improve education, which worsened; further emphasized by his commitment to send his daughter to private rather than public school, and the near doubling of drug usage by America's children during his first term in office (not to say having drug dealers as guests in the White House), the reality of the new era and the abuse of power exercised by the government, or, better said, those behind it, is that the government was defiantly lying to the people of the country.

It didn't take long for Clinton to move from his polished smooth talk, to why he sought me out.

"I never even heard of you, Noah, " he said. "When I was studying White House intelligence files, I didn't know who you were when I came across your name. It was inconceivable to me that a person who has acted as consultant to three U.S. Presidents is someone I never heard about."

"I don't know if "consultant" is the right term, Mr. President," I responded. "It's more or less what we have been doing. Talking."

"That's very modest of you, Noah. Nixon could have wound up selecting Ford because of you. You changed history right there. We may have been blinded longer than we were to what Japan was doing if it wasn't for you. You also were a catalyst to Reagan and Bush in 1983 for the Star Wars defense which, as you well know, saved lots of American lives, and which among other things, gave us an easy win in the Persian Gulf. The Stars Wars Defense, when made known to Gorbachev, was also the catalyst for perestroika and nuclear disarmament. I would say that just on these things, you should be as impressed with yourself as I am with you."

"Even though I can't return the compliment?"

"I pretty much know, Noah, that you are not a fan of mine, and I know why. You're free to feel as you do. However, when Jimmy Carter was President, he was a very religious, a very good and honorable man, but a very bad President."

Clinton paused to see if I had anything to say. I didn't.

"While you no doubt think little of me, and even assuming you are right for feeling that way, I have really accomplished a lot in office. Take a look at where we are today in the world. We are the supreme military and economic power. This has all happened under my watch."

"President Clinton, I don't want to be disrespectful to the President of the United States, but you believe in the ends justifying the means. Yes, we are the sole and supreme military and economic superpower. However, how did we achieve it? We have stifled all opposition, we have assumed indirect and nearly total control over all industrial and third world countries by having hand selected leaderships throughout the world. And for the few that still escape us, you are working on it day and night."

"But what is wrong with that, Noah? How can you fault our country from doing the very thing, which is making a better life for everyone around the world. In the past two decades these foreign countries wanted us to be the world's policemen, but they wanted us to be no more than that. When we were sinking economically, no one would put their hand in their pocket. No one would help us out of our jam, as they expected us, always, to help them out of theirs. We had to solve our own problems. And the only way we could do it was by getting them to cooperate. We had to swing carrots in front of them, and we decided why did we have to be beggars, when they themselves weren't big enough to help us without our need to ask, yet beg."

The President spoke persuasively. However, it was not the central issue.

"Mr. President, if you abuse power overseas to make sure the leadership is in line with the new world order, you can't wind up with a leader here at home out of sync with everything already put into place."

President Clinton, no doubt, knew what I was talking about. Reagan was put into line. Clinton was a willing participant. Now, what the true power behind the government had to watch out for were the Newt Gingrich types.

What was it that Gingrich said? That we can't go around fixing elections. David Rockefeller must have listened well, because instead of fixing our elections, we are just coyly limiting the candidates who run for office.

What does this mean? If you have two or three candidates, and regardless of their party designation, they subscribe to the new world order agenda, or are subject to its direct control, there's no need to fix elections. The power elite can get their favorite by slanting the media towards their favorite candidate. However, regardless of who wins, they win. This strategy is tantamount to large corporations donating to all candidates, so whomever wins, they have an access door available to them in Washington, not to say major influence. And while in years past, an American citizen could literally walk into the Senate office building and gain access to his elected representative, today you are first checked on a list of contributors: the smaller your contribution, the longer the wait, and possibly no access whatsoever.

The candidate Clinton ran against was the one he dreamt about getting the nomination: Bob Dole. Not that Dole wouldn't make a better President, but that Dole wasn't a candidate who stood much of a chance against media master Bill Clinton. And he didn't, as was spelled out clearly by Dick Morris, Clinton's infamous political strategist.

Dick Morris, said something very disturbing. He relayed that one of the great mysteries to him is why the Republicans, who were well financed, sat there on their hands, when he for critical months took out uncontested advertisements, which gave Clinton his original lead against Dole; a lead which Dole could never recover against, due to his lack of skills regarding media machinations.

Was Morris' inquiry a facade for a decision to place their agents into key positions within the Dole campaign? After all, when did anyone see such a poorly managed and orchestrated campaign? Was Robert Dole, Senate Majority Leader, acclaimed by his fellow Congressmen, Democrats and Republicans alike, for many years a sudden dunce? Or did he put his trust into people he should not have? Many of Dole's own Republican supporters wondered whether he was competent to run the country, if he couldn't run a campaign.

While Dole should have perhaps realized that his running against Clinton was parallel to Nixon running against Kennedy in 1960, Dole knew that no one could have better ammunition to undermine a President. Clinton was encompassed by a plethora of serious issues, which the media master was expert at derailing, delaying or avoiding altogether. Our founding fathers no doubt are restless in their eternal sleep knowing that a man with such a low moral profile as William Jefferson Clinton, regardless of his ability to operate in high office, would even have the nerve to run for office.

Of course, our founding fathers would have no firm idea how much the quality of simple honor has been eroded for the conquest of personal gain and glory. Damn be it that his fiduciary duty encompasses the welfare of the entire Nation and its people. Isn't that just how J.R. Ewing would look at it? Is Clinton emulating Kennedy or Ewing?

So I asked President Clinton: "Mr. President, are you willing to get up and go on national television and explain our true foreign policy? *Are you willing to answer me what the chances are that someone against existing U.S. policies, against the new world order, has of running or winning?*"

"You mean someone like Buchanan, Noah? Is that the candidate of your choice?"

"Of course he's not, Mr. President. But whether he is my choice or not, if the people for whatever reason want him to run, and he is elected, what happens to current U.S. policies?"

"They would be totally undermined. Everything I and the Presidents before me have accomplished would be ruined. If you knew that the interests of the United States would be compromised like that, how can you argue for Buchanan?"

"You see Mr. President. You are making me an extremist by using Buchanan as an example. Only an extremist, and those behind him, would be willing to destroy everything accomplished. What happens if a candidate, a very normal candidate, didn't believe in a global economy?

Would that alone make him an extremist?. Would that make him a person who shouldn't be allowed to run for office?"

"Noah, name me one instance where anyone has ever been denied the opportunity to run for office?"

"Name me one instance, Mr. President, of any candidate against existing policies that has run for office?"

The President knew a good counter when he heard one.

"Let me first ask you a question, Mr. President. Are you saying that the U.S. has not enmeshed itself in foreign elections? I take it you well know about my advertisement in the *Jerusalem Post.* Do you think your role in Israel was correct?"

"Is your concern about our policies towards foreign elections or domestic elections, " the President said trying to return the conversation to where he wanted it to go.

"Let me better make my point, sir. ***My point is that you can't go around fixing elections all over the planet and then pretend you are not going to carry that abuse of power back home.*** For example, I know that you are not going to allow everything accomplished vanish, by letting someone like Buchanan or Forbes, or Perot or Dole, get the nomination or the election, unless they are with your agenda or unless they can be brought into that agenda."

I continued, "And you know how that agenda was explained to Ronald Reagan."

President Clinton didn't touch that remark.

It was time for me to cut to the chase. "Mr. President why is it that you stopped to speak to me?"

"I am asking you Noah as President of the United States of America to turn over the TWA tapes you have."

The Meyersons, the couple from Carle Place, or cousin Robert must have talked, deliberately or inadvertently.

The President was now going to make it very clear to me how serious this matter was.

"The Meyersons are dead. They were killed when a stolen eighteen wheeler on 495 crashed into their car. There were five others killed in the accident."

It was certainly his way of telling me that he had the Meyerson copy of the full original. Was I in more danger than I thought? Were they going to kill me right there? Was cousin Robert still alive?

I tried to keep my cool. The President had caught me by surprise.

"Mr. President, in all due respect I know the Meyersons. They are friends of someone in my family. However, I do not know what you are referring to when you say TWA tapes."

"Noah, I am the President of the United States. I am asking for you to turn those tapes over to me."

I couldn't discuss the issues surrounding the tapes with the President. Doing so, would be an admission that I had them. However, I figured the government must have positively known I had them or else it wouldn't be using the President to make a case for them. The Meyerson tape must be the only known recording of the accident.

"Mr. President, as you said, I have spoken to many other Presidents before. I wouldn't lie to you. I don't know what you are talking about," keeping in mind that I was the Meyersons' attorney. I didn't officially know for sure whether they were dead, though I had no doubt about it.

My position was clear. The President made his position clear too. He stood up and left.

Why would I lie to the President of the United States? Why would I lie and deny the President of the United States what he asked for? Who the heck am I to think I have the right to do something like this?

After Playboy, after Dallas and Dynasty, we now faced a government who was moving to obtain total control of a free, open, and aggressive media and press. I was talking to a President who I didn't hold in the esteem he held himself. A President who should have had the character never to run for office, who has told Americans that they can spin the truth to improve their lives and create more opportunities for success; who allows the government to perpetuate an open bold, brazen lie. The government has gotten away with murder, including undermining our Constitution and country for so long, that government's disrespect and disdain for its citizens has become institutionalized as a course of government action.

Why couldn't and why wouldn't he as President of the United States tell the American public the truth about what was going on, about TWA Flight 800. I kicked myself for not asking him what I asked David Rockefeller. Why couldn't we solve our drug problem. Why did he repeatedly promise to save our children from drugs and stand so silently, like a church mouse, when drug use by children doubled during his watch. My idea of what William Jefferson Clinton accomplished during his watch is a lot different than his.

Bill Clinton, I concluded, didn't like me. I really didn't give a damn. A government that can boldly and brazenly lie regarding TWA Flight 800 is a government that cannot and should not be trusted. The silence of the press further supports this serious assertion.

I had severe problems now. I had to warn Robert, and I had to figure out what to do.

I called Robert and I told him to invite as many friends over as he could. I told him to call the local police and to hire two off duty cops round the clock until I got there.

When I got to New York, I called Robert and told him to have the off duty cops currently at his home to drive him to the New York Times building on West 45th Street.

During the hour and a half I was waiting for Robert at the Times Building, I found a young kid who was helping his father stack the papers onto his newspaper truck. While I had no doubt that the government knew I was in the building, I watched my surroundings fully to make sure no one was eyeballing me.

I told the father that I would pay him $500 if his son would pick up videotape for me that I needed right away for a presentation in the building. I took five $100 bills, tore them in half, and gave the father and the kid one half and told them I would give them the other half when he returned with the videotape.

The father said that if his son was picking up a videotape fine, but if there was anything else, a box, a package, or anything like that, his son wasn't going to touch it. I agreed. I gave the kid $50 to take a cab, but I told him he had to catch it north of 48th street, not anywhere around this building.

Agreed.

The kid took a cab to the Woolworth building, where downstairs I had taken a locker for a year under a fictitious name. Many attorneys and professionals used the facility, and the kid told the desk, when he got there, that he was picking it up for me, "Jason McGaw," that I left a videotape in my locker which I needed for a Mid-town meeting, already in progress. The management went with him, opened the locker, saw the videotape, which I labeled "Family Vacation Orlando 96," and the kid, in accordance with my instructions, went to the coffee shop on the first floor of the Woolworth building, bought a cup of coffee, asked for a bag, threw out the coffee, and put the videotape inside the bag.

When the kid returned with the bag, Robert was already there. He swore he never told anyone anything. Obviously the Meyersons talked.

Without question, the FBI, after conducting a thorough investigation of the videotape, discovered the edit. Using the other videotapes from the party, with their time stamps, which the Meyersons didn't have, the FBI concluded that the edited portion took place at the very time of the TWA Flight 800 incident. While the other videos faced immaterial directions, our video faced exactly the way it had to face to capture the actual accident.

I told Robert we had to get the story out in the open – immediately.

We went upstairs and asked for the managing editor. I should have known something was amiss, when we were immediately welcomed into his office, before he knew what we even had with us.

He swore us to secrecy, and called in his top two assistants. They told us that it would be front page probably within two days. They said it was going to be the story of the year.

They asked what we wanted in payment for the tapes. Despite Robert's protests, I convinced him to take nothing. After the President asked me for the tapes, I didn't want a spin that I lied to the President because I wanted to make money with them.

I coerced Robert to check in with me in a motel in Woodbridge, New Jersey. Robert didn't understand. I told him that until the story hit the papers, and played out we were better off being inaccessible. If we later wanted, we could discuss the issues with whomever we pleased.

When we left our second floor motel room at 6:00 PM for dinner, two shots rang out. Robert died immediately. He was hit squarely in the neck. I knew right then that the *New York Times* would never use the tape.

I was hit in the shoulder. I lunged into the room and called 911.

I thought the assassin or assassins would surely burst in. I kicked myself for not having a weapon.

The reason I called 911 was because I knew the assassin(s) would be monitoring the police broadcasts and no doubt due to who I thought they were, the 911 exchange.

I next called the front desk. Henry Raymous, the front desk manager was there, and I offered him $1000 cash for an immediate car ride to Scarsdale, New York.

Henry Raymous told his assistant that he had a family emergency, and three minutes later I was bleeding all over Henry's ten-year-old Nissan. He didn't say a word. One thousand dollars for an hour and a half drive would silence a lot of people.

In Scarsdale, my good friend, treated me. I told my doctor friend that he wouldn't be seeing me ever again. I was sorry because my being there was going to cause him a lot of grief. I told him it was better that I told him nothing else.

I had Henry Raymous wait, and gave him another $200 for dropping me in Midtown, Manhattan. There I waved down a cab, which took me to Allentown Avenue in the Bronx. I knew someone who would keep me out of the picture until I recovered.

CHAPTER 17
THE LIMOUSINE RIDE

I didn't need to access machine intelligence systems to know whom to blame.

All my work, and my research, all my systems were now in the hands of the FBI. While all my work was encrypted, with the Rockefeller nod, decrypting them was possible with the aid of the government's best supercomputers. While otherwise, the encryption algorithms I used would take from ten to one hundred years or more to decrypt, with the government's computers they would do it within a year, and with luck, three months.

They had won the war. They lost no one, and completely neutralized me, my attempts to correct the course for the country, my evidence, and now without it costing them a legitimate cent, they would have my work.

I could hear George Bush saying, "Noah, we would never admit to anything. And if the *New York Times* had published a story concerning your videotape, we would have applauded it. We would have said that we and the families of the victims are totally relieved at finally knowing the truth. Nothing else would have changed. Why in the world would you ever think you could overtake us on our agenda?"

They knew my profile. They knew I was a religious person and did not believe in murder. Else I would be like those I purported to oppose. However, they did not discount my ability to turn bad. When hunted and hounded, when you know you are going to die, when you know you have failed, and when you know you have no future, and evil has prevailed, you can prove to be an exception to your own profile.

And I certainly was.

As you must understand, I could never prove anything in any court of law against David Rockefeller. I had however a very clear conscience about what I was going to do.

I was a marked man. I knew that there would be no way to escape my fate unless I covertly left the country and hid out for the rest of my life. To encourage this result, the government issued a warrant for my arrest. It appears that the police found drugs at the motel room where Robert and I were staying, waiting for the *New York Times* to disclose the news about the TWA video.

Henry Raymous became a government witness, and, for unknown consideration, made up a story that had me in the drug business. His version was that I put a gun to his head to take him to Scarsdale.

My physician friend, now finding himself known as treating a wanted drug dealer, and to top it off, his personal friend as well, lost a lot of his community stature. I am sure he forgives me, realizing that the only alternative for me was death.

I had no doubt that the powers I was up against would prevail, especially since I didn't want to take up residence in a remote area of Mexico or South America. Even there, I was sure that my days were numbered.

However, if I was going to go, if my future was now worthless, I was going to take David Rockefeller with me. He knew it and thus the search for me was intense.

I traveled up to Schuyler county and through old contacts bought some military C4 and Detasheet from a militia group. The one thing about plastic explosives is that it can be formed into almost any shape.

When you want to assassinate someone, it's simple these days with the technologies available. You can buy mapping software and get the longitude or latitude of anyone's home you are interested in targeting, build a model airplane with C4 explosive, set a trigger device to actuate when your intercepts are reached by the plane, and if your target is within 50 feet of the explosion, you have succeeded, even if the target, like David Rockefeller was within the confines of the gates of his estate.

However, this was a methodology I had mentioned to clients throughout the years, and without question, David Rockefeller was ready for it.

My plan was to travel up to North Tarrytown and determine as a reporter what were his favorite haunts in town. Does he stop for anything on a routine basis? Did he have a favorite restaurant, a favorite table? Was there a doctor, dentist, friend, shop, person, mayor, or anyone else he routinely visited as part of his family's residence in the area?

Where was his family buried? Was there a graveside he visited routinely and regularly on a specific day or time? Was there a street he always passed through? Did he walk outside the gates of his estate? Did he go to a regular favorite restaurant in New York? Did he have a regular table there? Where was his hair cut?

Did he go to church? Where and how often? Did he have a steady pew? Where did his children live? Did he visit them or grandchildren routinely?

Where was his plane hangered? Where did his limousine routinely stop? How far is it between the plane and limousine?

Where are his cars serviced? Did he have steady drivers? Did he have any disgruntled employees? Where were they? Whom could he talk to in pursuing his assignment as a reporter? Who previously worked for David Rockefeller and now worked elsewhere?

Somewhere there is an opening. People within his community, from his postman to his church, to those attending his church, to the neighborhood local businessmen, to those working at his estate, to those previously working at his estate, to the friends or classmates of his children or grandchildren, would provide the information which would create the opening.

What was I planning on doing?

Preferably you find a restaurant where he routinely likes to eat. You place strips of C4 under the table. No one checks restaurant tables for explosives. You wait. One day, your target will come into his restaurant and be seated at his favorite table. You walk in with a disguise, or have someone else, for a price, walk in; push a button on a remote, and the rest is history.

While moving about in Tarrytown with a disguise on, to get the answers I needed, I recognized my friend and fellow tenant from the town house on 27th and P. I hadn't seen him in thirty years. He didn't act as though he knew anything about my arrest warrant or claims that I was involved in the drug trade. He wouldn't have stopped to talk to me. He did ask me when I identified myself, why I was wearing an apparent disguise.

I told him I was doing an investigative piece on David Rockefeller, and he looked at me forlornly as though I hadn't accomplished much in life, working as a reporter for a newspaper. He asked which, and I told him the *New York Times*.

Since he was from a very rich and connected family, I thought he might know what I was there to find out. He invited me to go with him to his family estate, and I gladly accepted. It was nice to see him.

However, after I got in to the back of his 1937 Rolls Royce limousine, and saw what I first thought was his body guards, it struck me, with the subtle visible change of his body language, that I had fallen into a trap. I was caught.

William, my old Georgetown friend, sat across from me, while I sat surrounded by the two bodyguards, who were very serious looking fellows.

"William, I am getting the feeling that my accidental bumping into you today was no accident at all."

"Correct, Noah," he replied. "We have much to discuss."

"You are looking at your guardian angel, Noah," William continued. "You really should have been dead long ago. It never crossed your mind, did it Noah, that you've been exceptionally lucky?"

I didn't know what William was talking about. William continued:

"Nixon knew I lived at the town house. That's the reason he stopped. Out of respect for me. I heard about your being in the motorcade. We laughed about it when I went with Nixon to California to see Patty. So when he saw you outside the townhouse that night, he stopped, and inadvertently changed history."

Nixon, on behalf of William's family, had set him up with Patty Hearst. This was in 1969, before she gained her notoriety.

I was taken aback. I was confused. I felt I was in dire danger. But I couldn't understand what was happening or why.

"What is it, that you're telling me, William?"

"I'm telling you Noah that I have been your guardian angel since the time I have first known you. I liked you. I wasn't kidding when I said you would have had it made, if you weren't Jewish. You would have married my sister, and we would have been family."

I still was totally mixed up. "So why were you my guardian angel?"

"You have to understand Noah that my grandfather and Nelson and David Rockefeller's grandfather were long time friends. With all modesty, their grandfather, as powerful as he was, held my grandfather in highest esteem."

"Who was your grandfather?"

"Kaiser Wilhem."

"Kaiser Wilhem of Germany?"

"Yes," William proudly responded.

I didn't know what to say next.

William continued: "They both were founders of what became in the early 50s, the Bilderberg group. They were setting up the agenda, the one which so disturbs you."

"However, as you surely know," he went on, "my family was pushed out of Germany when the fascists took over the country. However, that doesn't mean that my family ever relented from any intention   to recapture their rightful place."

"Which is?" I asked.

"To rule," William simply said. "We know how to run not only a country but as you have been so astutely following, the world."

I had to ask William, "Are you on top of Rockefeller or vice-versa – or are you equal partners, or are there more people involved?"

"You have been a very fortunate man, Noah. You know the top players. David is exposed to the public, but no one knows of me and my family, and the role we have played through the Rockefeller family here in America. We have been mentors to the Rockefeller family since the days of his grandfather."

William could see that my mind was feeble at absorbing the shocking revelations he was telling me.

"Look Noah. Your nine lives are up. Since fate brought you together with me, and I liked you so much, I had a strong desire to protect you. Not only did I protect you – I had so many golden opportunities presented to you, that even you must have recognized you were one of the luckiest people around.

"Since you're not totally stupid, I was befuddled for years why you acted like the stupidest man I have ever known."

"However, when you obtained possession of the TWA tapes, then you were making life difficult for me and others."

"Perhaps then you can tell me, William, why the government finds it necessary to lie about TWA Flight 800. What is really going on?"

"First, Noah, I want you to answer a question."

"What is it?"

"Today is a very important day for you. You have to decide whether you will come to my side and have a life you deserved long ago, or whether you want to continue refusing it. If you refuse it, you will not leave this limousine alive."

I knew William wasn't kidding.

"I want you to answer the TWA question first, William."

He looked at me and decided to comply.

"You are trying to save a country which is beyond redemption, Noah. Don't you see how many people today have no future, don't possess the qualities previous generations of Americans possessed."

"Well, Noah, in thirty to fifty years at the utmost," William continued, "whites will be a minority in America. Not only to blacks, but to Hispanics, Asians, Vietnamese, and a host of people who are already clamoring against English as the dominant language."

"With your approval," I couldn't resist interjecting.

"Good, Noah. Stupid you are not, as I said. We are just moving things along."

"But why?"

"Look, Noah, Europe at one time ruled, and my family ruled Europe. Those who fled the European countries, fled to America. They were considered to be second-rate European citizens. These second-rate citizens founded what turned out to be today's superpower country, one who defeated my family in the very early part of the century.

"But only you will appreciate this, Noah. It was my plan that brought the U.S. to its present status in the world. My family always knew that a country founded by second-rate citizens, would be susceptible to attack from within. So even before we had to leave Germany, we established a beachhead here and knew we could be the ones to take over covertly from within: particularly under the umbrella of the Rockefeller family."

"How long has this been going on."

"Since the 30s. But we have the providence of patience and knowing when we can move on our agenda. We are willing to wait, generations if necessary, for the right time and opportunity."

"You had nothing to do with the Kennedy assassination, did you?"

"Absolutely not. It was confirmation that America was vulnerable from within. Once Nixon was in, we were in place. However, Nixon wasn't really one of us: that is why we desperately wanted Nelson to take the Presidency. Ironical as it was, you influenced him to break his deal with Nelson."

"Why didn't you stop me from seeing him in 1973?"

"We couldn't. Your talk with him at the townhouse, and little did I know what you were going to talk to him about, made an impression of how well you understood the intrigue of power politics." After a pause, William also said: "I told him it was a benefit of spending so much time around me."

"So what were you doing in Washington at law school?"

"I was there to spend some time with regular people like you, Noah. I really never had much conversation during my life with middle class people, and I never spent any time at all with anyone Jewish."

It's nice getting a compliment and insult at the very same time.

"Why all the Jews around government today, William?"

"For my family, Noah, Jews have served a historical role, perhaps a biblical role, as scapegoats. If we have any problems, who are the masses going to blame? The Jews are a buffer for us. It's nothing personal, Noah. You have to understand that when my family ruled Germany, and we got into economic problems, and the Jews didn't do as an excuse, we would start a war with a neighboring country, sacrificing our own, to keep the people's minds off any blame at our door. Managing a nation is a very difficult task."

"You seem cold, dispassionate, heartless, in everything you say."

"You can't rule a nation, for the long term, and have a heart. You have to have a memory. This time my family will not make a mistake. We are not going to let any extremist come into the picture. We are not to be challenged. We control the media. We have the public totally absorbed by television and sports. We want to control who is in the military. We want a military that obeys orders and doesn't question if they are ordered to shoot citizens of their own country. We don't want a knowledgeable citizenry. We don't want the citizens to entertain any thought or hope that they can change things. We want them to understand that they must accept things as they are and adjust the best they can to how things are to provide themselves with a better edge and life to that of their neighbor. In short, Noah, you have been right about everything. . . .."

"Even that you intend to abandon this country down the road?"

"Of course. We used its strength and we will let it fall on its weakness as we re-establish Europe as the location for the future world government.

Did you think for a moment that my family did all this not to return to control Germany and take our rightful place there. Our destiny has been a great one, because not only will we get back control of our own country, we will get the rest of the world as a prize."

"What about the Rockefellers?"

"It's a big world Noah. We couldn't run it ourselves. When it comes to planning, it's just about over in another ten years. Then it's long term implementation and control, two things the Rockefellers specialize in."

"All those people in the councils have been used?"

"By their very involvement," William answered. "They are among the elite – the mutual admiration society whom appease each other. The elite always do everything and anything to continue their status, and will do anything asked to preclude being shunned as an elite insider."

"Like sell their souls?" I sarcastically said.

"Sure they sell their souls. People will sell a lot more than their souls. We and the Rockefellers are the providers of what they want. We are leaders. We are rulers."

"I thought David Rockefeller was a benevolent monarch. Now I see the both of you are benevolent dictators, aren't you William?"

"No, Noah, we are the best for the world. While you were right what you told David, that we are using the country for our own agenda, we are better than the alternative: war, nuclear war, global devastation, conflict, turmoil."

"Please, Noah. I haven't said please to anyone in many years. But please, come with us. You don't have to speak for us. Just stop working against us. Strange that fate brought me a person I like who has proven to be a putative opponent."

"And strange is fate, William ,who brought me a guardian angel, who is my enemy."

"How can you call me an enemy, Noah? That angers me. I have been your friend. I am your friend. Why do you act so stupidly and stubbornly? Please, Noah, just tell me, give me your word that you will stop. Turn over any other copies of the TWA tape. Tell me what you need and want, so I can provide them for you, and they will be yours."

"William, I know you believe that you are being wonderful to me. But my answer is based on the following.

"You know most of my family died during WWII under Hitler. My father shared few stories with me, but he wrote many of them down in Yiddish and I had them translated into English after he passed on.

"One of those stories involved a non Jewish civilian who approached a woman and her daughter before they were to be herded into a cattle car to the death camps. The civilian told the mother that he wanted to marry her beautiful daughter. He would save her from death.

"The mother refused saying that she would defile God's name and her family by permitting such a marriage to take place. Her daughter would face the same fate as her family. The mother and her daughter were taken to the death camps.

"For all my life, I always criticized the mother for not saving her daughter. If she agreed, her daughter would live. She was, to my mind, the direct cause of her death. After the war, the daughter could have divorced or taken steps to break away from the man, if she so desired. I thought the mother was wrong, until today.

"And now, William, while everyone else probably would thank you for being "so generous," it would involve selling my soul, compromising what I believe in. I would knowingly stop working against something which I think is wrong – essentially prostituting my life, my convictions, as that fellow wanted that young beautiful girl to do, to save her life. As much as I thought the mother wrong till today, I now know how right she was in making the decision for her daughter. My answer is no."

With that, William pushed a button on the console on his arm rest, a needle came out of the back of my seat, directly into my back, injecting me with a dose of some substance which thirty seconds later ended my life.

As I was fading off from life, I could hear William saying one last thing to me: "Noah, you are the biggest fool I have known in my life. But a fool I have always admired. While you haven't changed the course I am on, you have done good for what you believe in – for you, and your death, by my own hand, will remain with me the remainder of my life, and your life will have, as it has had, meaning."

Noah Guerin was buried beside his father in Woodbridge, New Jersey. There, at his funeral, in front of a simple gravesite, stood William, with his beautiful wife, Katherine, known to Noah as Christine, speaking to David Rockefeller about finally cracking Noah's machine intelligence systems, and what it would mean to them in the future.

Also standing near Katherine, were her three children. Standing to her left, was her eldest son, William Jr. 22 years old, heir apparent to her husband's power, wealth, and family dynasty. William Jr. to everyone there, but her husband, was the spitting image to the person lying in the closed coffin: the enduring memory to "Christine" of her trip and mission to Acapulco, Mexico in 1973.

Noah's Rabbi stood completely dumbfounded in seeing three Presidents of the United States – President Reagan, himself ill, President Bush, and President Clinton – standing beside Henry Kissinger, Conrad Black and a host of other dignitaries, attending a funeral of a man the Rabbi really didn't know: one who his congregation told him was a drug dealer, and who died the death of one.

The Rabbi in speaking about Noah Guerin started by saying, in view of his distinguished audience, "We are here to pay final respects to a great man, however, I must admit…that while Noah Guerin, without question, was a great man, I myself, have no idea why."

The End

W hile Noah Guerin died, his messages haven't.:

The Kennedy Assassination.: Nearly every American has recognized that he or she has been lied to.

Americans trusted their government. If there was a reason to lie to the public, American citizens could tolerate it from a government that they could trust.

However, any basis for trust has evaporated, and now the deliberate passivity of the American public to demanding the truth about the Kennedy assassination, wrongfully serves as the basis of institutionalized lying and deceit by government to those it purports to represent.

The Nixon Presidency was really a platform for the American public to see the intricate web between the media and political office.

Very few Americans can remember the original passivity of the press toward the Watergate incident, or the obvious machination of political forces to quickly and expeditiously remove Spiro Agnew from office, with Richard Nixon's ultimate decision to refuse to appoint his original first choice, Nelson Rockefeller, Vice-President of the United States of America.

When Nixon named Gerald Ford, history shows the diametrically opposite unbridled aggressiveness of the media in pursuing the Watergate story, resulting in Richard Nixon's resignation from the Presidency of the United States of America.

Why would Nelson Rockefeller in 1976 shy away from running as Vice-President, if it weren't to attest that he lost in his campaign to secure the Presidency for himself and his family; for it would be too late for him in 1980. As it was, he died in 1979.

The message here, combined with the putative dynamics behind the Kennedy assassination, is that American politics have been subject to the same forces and battles for power attendant to all other foreign states and countries, including third world nations.

Thus, the evident and dire need for the media to be open, vigilant, aggressive and independent; and the message of why those who covertly seek power, need to manage and control it.

The Reagan Administration attested to the victory of forces of pure self-centered capitalism over democracy itself.

This was evidenced by the very fact that a popular figure and President, Ronald Reagan, who otherwise wasn't known for being weak or timid, came under the control and grasp of the forces fighting for inside control of the United States of America.

Reagan had firm economic programs, strategies and philosophies in mind, when he took office, all which vanished after he was nearly killed by the bullets of John Hinckley.

Thereafter again, the American people showed their reliance on government and the media by again trusting these two entities, intentionally covering the assassination attempt as nothing more than the isolated sociopath deed of a deranged individual.

This may have been fine and true, but for the fact of the dramatic changes in President Reagan's programs, strategies and philosophies, immediately after the assassination attempt.

Further couple this with the fact of whom would have been President if Hinckley's bullets met a fatal mark: George Bush, from a family long aligned with the programs, policies and philosophies of the one-world government agenda.

During Reagan's tenure, under the umbrella of Reagan's name and past philosophies, the new elitist centrix rooted themselves into control of the country, and then used the country to establish its agenda throughout the world.

While Noah Guerin always knew that George Bush was the prime public representative of the elitist centrix, he also knew that Bush himself also was very sensitive to the evil behind the covert leaders of this group.

That was the reason Noah believed George Bush chose Dan Qualye as his Vice-President. What was obvious to Noah Guerin was a mystery to others. George Bush gave himself added insurance that what happened to others would not happen to him. He had been around too long to ever believe that he was guaranteed complete safety, regardless of whether he was a favorite son of the elitist centrix.

Nevertheless, George Bush during his four years, let the elitist centrix gain complete control and power over the media and other institutions, and pursuant to the game plan, masked the reality of what was going on by manipulating policies, including the Federal Reserve, to establish the longest bull market in world history, combined with artificially low interest rates.

Antitrust laws and other fundamental protections against monopolies went by the wayside, as dominant corporations, with a nexus to the elitist centrix, took control over all the media, outside of newsprint, who were already in friendly hands. This control went from within the U.S. to the media and newspapers throughout the world.

George Bush showed the world who was the military force to be reckoned with: the elitist centrix, through the U.S., took control over Russia, made material gains in China, getting U.S. interests and operatives enmeshed into the national framework, and took control over the Mid-East.

Bush, in his second term, was ready to take on the economic juggernaut of Japan, and without reason, to the dismay of James Baker, his Secretary of State, and chief co-executioner of elitist centrix policies and programs, he just failed to do what was necessary to win the election.

Further, Noah Guerin always believed that James Baker tried to urge George Bush to manipulate the election results here at home; but that Bush, ironically like Gorbachev and Rabin, would not go as far as the new morality of the elitist centrix encouraged. He couldn't himself sleep if he knew he took the Presidential election by stealth.

However, if he were in George Bush's shoes, **William Jefferson Clinton** would never share such perceived pangs of conscience.

The elitist centrix after doing everything they could to at first help promote Clinton as a failure, thereafter did everything to restore him, when he became their best soldier, reaping the highest rewards in not only taking on Japan, but sending forth the elitist centrix morality to fix elections and candidates in nearly every important country on the planet, including Israel and Russia.

Noah Guerin before he was killed spoke unceasingly about what is taking place in England, where the elitist centrix must win.

Thus, the unexpected heart attack of Majors former foe, John Smith, and the role now assumed by Clinton clone, Tony Blair. Consequently, whoever wins, Majors or Blair, the elitist centrix agenda is intact.

This openly successfully scored scenario of elitist centrix forces, portended, to Noah, the future of American politics and the need to convey his story and messages.

Nothing however distressed and concerned Noah more than **TWA Flight 800**. The entire episode to Noah was a test case of how far the elitist centrix had come into control, how much they eviscerated the soul and spirit of the American public, how they could implicate and obtain further control over once independent government agencies, and how successful they were going to be when they pulled out the rug from the United States of America, and made it only one part of the new federation of world states, which the elitist centrix would completely control, to establish new laws and policies governing the entire planet and which laws and policies no doubt couched under an aura of purported democratic and capitalistic principles, would mask their awarding themselves control and power in perpetuity.

What, if by the time you read this book, the government has convinced you that something else caused TWA Flight 800 to go down? The message and issue is whether you as an American citizen are being treated with dignity and respect. *There is no national interest in hiding something already shown on television: the six to eight seconds of radar images.* However, there is a serious problem when the FBI keeps all the evidence locked up from everyone else. There is serious issue when the media finds itself pushing the government agenda rather than unraveling for the American public facts and issues known to many intelligent people throughout the world. It's almost like it is a test of how far they can push the envelope, for future reference. In other words, how dumb and stupid and how much will the American public swallow. If a great deal, then they can just conclude that when the new world order capital moves out of the United States that the American public, raped and misused for so long, will, as all victims, be with little resolve or energy to speak up or out against an overwhelming power and force the government will be by that ugly day. On such a day, Americans will be totally impotent. However, that day is not today.

Are you desensitized to all the lies, secrets and deceptions; the crime and violence; the drug situation; the educational problems; the lack of respect of children for parents, the lack of religion, morals, values ethics, in government and in society?

Do you feel powerless and impotent to effectuate change?

Would you like things to change? Would you like open, honest, truthful government, with politicians who are out for you not themselves?

The first issue is a very simple and clear one. You want a President and other national leadership who will rid America of drugs.

The dynamic, which establishes the value of this book and its assertions, is as follows. We have a government that can take out Japan, and become the sole superpower in the world. This same government has not successfully eradicated drugs from within its borders, and stands by, almost silently, as drug usage dramatically increases and becomes mainstay among the children of our nation. This same government also fails on every promise to improve the educational structure for our nation, and despite billions flowing in from lotteries, it allows education to continue to fall into a darker and wider abyss. These facts, standing alone, support that something is going on inconsistent with the interests of the American citizen and his family.

Thus, until you see a politician, preferably a President of the United States, who removes this drug scourge from this Nation, you can firmly accept the underlying tenets upon which the message of this book is delivered: corrupt government with a hidden power element/group acting inapposite to the interests of this Nation.

How can the drug scourge be successfully dealt with?

Politicians like corporations, are chameleons, who can turn into saints if their existence depends upon it. And perhaps if *Recapturing America* can engender some attention, that someone will get up and do something about it now.

Americans want drugs away from their children. At the time of the TWA Flight 800 explosion, it was reported that drug use by 13-14 year olds went from 11% in 1991 to 23% in 1996. This single fact shows you what Bill Clinton, his war on drugs, is all about: a facade. The simple strategy: we want your commitment to rid America from drugs in two years, or you're out, *turns the dynamic to what a politician does, not what he says. It doesn't allow for excuses. Americans should no longer give any quarter, when it comes to the resolution of the drug plague on America and its children.*

If a candidate doesn't agree to a two year term, if he isn't successful in ridding the nation of 80%+ of drugs, then you don't want him. You want to convey what you want and then you want to make sure that they deliver.

A possible strategy is to fight fire with fire by harnessing the most powerful resources we have in America to help eliminate the problem. The U.S. corporation exists by privilege. It has no right to exist. So if it follows the guidelines provided for its existence, it can exist. Otherwise, its privilege to exist can be expunged.

We need guidelines, because corporations by their very nature exist solely for profit. If you had no guidelines, corporations would be involved in all sorts of illegal activities to perpetuate the purpose of their existence: profit. However, to exist and continue to exist, they must conduct business legally and otherwise follow the guidelines provided. The reason they so willingly oblige is because if they fail to follow the guidelines, they cannot exist.

So if we told corporations that to exist the CEO each morning had to help a little old lady cross a street in their town, do you know what? No matter how wealthy this CEO is and no matter how much he makes in salary and bonus, and no matter how little time he has on his schedule, you can bet your bottom dollar that he will help a little old lady each and every morning cross the street.

Likewise, we can direct a condition that unless the corporations of America, working alone or together, eliminate the drug scourge in America, that in two years they will have a 35% tax surcharge until the condition is resolved. There, of course, will be an outcry but, believe me, all my experience with government, corporations and people make it very clear, to my mind, that when you employ the resources of American industry working on an issue, including their vast local and national contacts, that chances are they will succeed. You have to give them incentive and when it's all over, we all will be winners.

You want candidates who truly oppose one another on major issues. You want candidates who speak the truth, who tell you what road this country is on, and whom you can trust. You can always trust people who are givers, not takers, and if the media and press do their job, rather than serve as pawns for the powers behind government, they would tell you who they are.

If government intimidates the media, then the wrong people are in government and the wrong people are in the media. You want strong people to stand up to government, and you want people in government who do not punish people or companies, if they do not fall into line, by threatening policies or Congressional actions against their interests.

Noah's story aspires to activate the good in people currently in government, who know that there is a great deal of truth in the disturbing issues raised by this book. They have to stand up and self-sacrifice, and do their part to change things, because they are in a position to help effectuate change by making hidden problems, openly known problems.

As long as the drug problem remains, institutionalized corruption will endure and so will the disturbing issues raised by this book. Don't target anything else until success is reached in ridding the country of drugs.

Even before education, there is a need to deal with the abhorrent failure of the Federal Communications Commission to represent the public.

Those on the FCC sit in manifest representation of the public interest and good, but, they have brazenly, in the name of commercialism and profit, and self-centered capitalism, under the excuse of free speech and economic competition, bent the minds of the children of this country and desensitized Americans to important and disturbing issues. **Their crimes are far worse than some of our most hardened criminals, for they have impacted far more victims.** The following quote from one news story cuts the point in stone:

> Sixth-graders charged with trying to poison teacher.
>
> SAN BERNARDINO, Calif, May 15 (Reuter) - Two sixth-grade girls have been arrested and charged with spiking their teacher's Gatorade drink with rat poison while their classmates watched, authorities said on Wednesday.
>
> Two boys who allegedly hid the emptied box of poison were charged as accessories to the crime. Another student in the class warned the 54-year-old teacher before she drank it. The exact motive was not known, but the San Bernardino Sheriff's Department said in a statement that ``it is suspected that one of the girls may have been failing'' in her classwork.
>
> The incident began on Friday when a 12-year-old girl is alleged to have brought the rat poison to class at a middle school in Lucerne Valley, a small desert town about 65 miles (110 km) northeast of Los Angeles. Another girl, an 11-year-old classmate, grabbed their teacher's bottle of Gatorade drink while her back was turned and the 12-year-old poured the poison into it and placed it back on the teacher's desk, authorities said. Two boys then removed a vent cover and stashed the box of poison, the sheriff's department said
>
> ``She looked in the bottle and did see that the
>
> Gatorade didn't look normal,'' said a sheriff's department spokeswoman. At least 15 other students witnessed the act and one of them warned the teacher Sondra Haille not to drink it.
>
> The girls were charged with felony food poisoning and the boys with being accessories after the fact, also a felony. Chemical tests

were being conducted to determine whether the amount of poison would have made the drink lethal.

Government cannot control action, by simply passing laws, making one a felon for violating the law. *You control action by instilling values, and then teaching children that it is wrong to do it. The issue is not whether they go to jail, but whether they are able to know the difference between right and wrong. Television today desensitizes children from knowing the difference.* If you get mugged, you want a mugger who is questioning what he is doing, not one who is figuring the odds for and against a short or long jail term.

To be clear, this country protects first amendment rights, free speech and everything attendant to what was intended to be encompassed by the Constitution. However, restrictions in the use of the national airwaves, and in fact broadcast licenses are proffered in the name of public interest and the public good, are not per se proscriptions against the mandate of the U.S. Constitution.

Thus, programming which undermines respect of children for their parents, that implants violence to such a degree that children kill each other and find comfort in the use of guns and other sociopath releases, is criminal. Likewise, to instill the type of mind set, as in the children above, that to eliminate a problem, you can commit murder or do bodily harm, is criminal. This wasn't one person acting; other children were involved including hiding the poison in a vent in a desire to emulate the type of behavior glamorized by television programming. The saddest part of the news report is that only one child stopped the crime, among a class of fifteen, *and our point is that soon this single child will be history, meaning there will be not even one child who will speak out and warn the teacher, and we will have children murdering their teachers. This, not to discount, the current day reality of teachers fearful for their lives and welfare.*

Broadcast of adult entertainment is not encompassed as a first amendment right. The Constitution asserts that you cannot limit its availability for those who want it, but it doesn't pretend to guarantee that it must be given a guarantee of delivery via the public airwaves. Individuals, including parents insensitive to this perspective, can go out and buy or rent whatever kind of entertainment they want in their homes. However, the national airwaves are not a medium for distribution of all facets of putative entertainment. There is a fiduciary duty to the American citizen and American family over any other consequence: economic or otherwise. That is why licenses to operate on them are given only to those who agree to serve the public interest and good. Desensitization, like any other injury, to children is always contrary to the public interest and good and thus contrary to the public trust. If any politician today has a dispute with this, please, let's put it on the ballot and see what the American people have to say about it.

Corporations, if within the guidelines, will do anything for profit. So if you don't preclude them from improperly bending children's minds to sell their products or wares, they don't care about the impact on children: they care about whether it is effective for increased sales of the product.

Each network and competitor says they have to devise competitive programming and thus no one is going to move away from sex, crime and violence if others are going to employ it and be more successful than they. It is against their corporate responsibilities. And they are correct. So, the overriding fiduciary responsibility has to be discharged by the representatives of the people: those on the Federal Communications Commission. They have failed miserably. They have sacrificed our children.

Moreover, it's not sufficient for you to find solace that you might be among Americans who are happy with their financial situation, and thus expediently conclude that you don't have serious problems. If the fabric of this country is being undermined, you have serious problems. Whether your financial situation is real or just perhaps an illusion long term, is secondary, to the point of this book that you are responsible for the future environment your children will live and exist in.

We don't want them to be desensitized to the values of honesty, character and self-sacrifice. We don't want to see them successful because they can simply spin the truth, manipulate others, and arrange major machinations of people and things, to win and to profit. What kind of people will we become? Look at our children today.

If you carry the messages of Noah Guerin in your mind, you will help effectuate change. The politicians will ultimately get the message and the current ones, as the chameleons they are, will change and provide the first steps towards the recapture of control over our own government.

Collectively, there is no greater power than you and your fellow Americans sending signal out for change.

The following are revealing excerpts from the world media, with comments reflecting the author's opinion thereon.

First keep the following in mind:

The powers behind this government used the resources of this Nation to capture world domination, but simultaneously allowed the collapse in important segments of the domestic infrastructure. Why would they? How could they allow the U.S. to fall as we have domestically? It doesn't make sense, and it points to the underlying message of this book. You can't have the talent and resources to control the world, and say you are unable to solve the drug and education problems of your own nation, unless you don't want to, or for some reason don't care enough to.

In September, 1996, David Rockefeller gave an address where he said:

"... unless business accepts the challenge of helping to solve the many societal problems, education, drugs, crime, inadequate housing, I am concerned that the political pendulum may swing back and that many of our fellow citizens may become disenchanted with business and demand that government reassume its previous role as the arbiter of our economic life. Our current election campaign has provided many examples of the strength that such populist sentiments still enjoy throughout the country."

Comment: This is David Rockefeller acknowledging that the control of the government is in the hands of business, his constituency of elitists, and while they are living the good life in all respects, he is proffering his wisdom, that a populist movement can arise which will undermine all achieved.

He is saying that while corporations exist for profit and gain, they must develop the facade of social responsibility to foreclose attack for failing to address domestic problems, which are not otherwise primary concerns of the elitists whom he addresses. In this very regard, David Rockefeller said:

"In other words, big business today, as it was in my grandfather's time in the early 1900s and quite frequently in the years since, is once again "suspect." And corporate leaders, primarily due to downsizing, are once again widely distrusted. As one commentator recently put it, "Americans are suspicious that a rising tide may, in fact, lift all the yachts, but sink all the rowboats!"'"

Rockefeller knows from whenst he speaks. In the May 14, 1995 edition of the *Los Angeles Times*, the following was written in an article entitled, "MEXICO 75 Years Later, Today's Zapatistas Still Fight the Rockefeller Legacy," acknowledging the relationship of Nelson and David Rockefeller to Mexico and the NAFTA agreement:"

"Like Zapata in his criticism of the Carranza regime of his time, the Zapatistas see the government of President Ernesto Zedillo as doing the bidding of foreign companies.

They believe that U.S. oil companies seek to regain control of Mexico's oil, lost *since the holdings of the Rockefellers' Standard Oil and other U.S. firms were nationalized, in 1937,* by President Lazaro Cardenas.

They note that Mexico's oil revenues have been put up as collateral for the $49-billion bailout arranged by the Clinton Administration. They also note the involvement of large foreign banks in speculating in the pre-NAFTA Mexican stock market, key among them Chase, whose retired CEO, David Rockefeller, has been the trailblazer for NAFTA ever since his brother Nelson, vice president in the Ford Administration, died in 1979.

Nelson A. Rockefeller had fostered U.S. corporate investment in Latin America since the 1930s, when he was a director of Standard Oil of New Jersey's Venezuelan subsidiary and tried to negotiate a settlement with President Cardenas for Standard in Mexico. In the 1940s, Rockefeller set up the Mexican American Development Corp. and was a personal investor in Mexican industries after the war, encouraging his brother David to set up Chase's Latin America division. As chairman of the International Development Advisory Board, Rockefeller became the architect of President Harry S.Truman's foreign-aid program, using U.S. guarantees to leverage the massive lending by Chase, Citicorp and other banks that would result in the Mexican people assuming a $120-billion foreign debt, with $18.3 billion owed directly to the U.S. banks. The inability of Mexico to pay these debts was recognized long ago and answered by Rockefeller's proposal for a hemispheric free-trade zone that would keep trade and the financial bubble growing.

It was in 1959 when Nelson Rockefeller, testing the feasibility of a presidential bid with a national speaking tour only one year after being elected governor of New York, visited Southern California and Texas and called for a hemispheric "economic federation" of free trade that was the harbinger of NAFTA. Today, Rockefeller's legacy lives with us in the economic integration of Mexico into NAFTA and the crisis this has triggered in Mexico. One of the key conditions for Mexico's entry into the NAFTA "dollar zone" was a change in Mexico's constitution that included ending prohibitions against the sale of ejidos-farms owned communally by Indian villagers according to ancient custom-to private interests and the phasing out of government subsidies for farmers. In effect, this will mean the sale of 30,000 ejidos to private companies. It was Zapata who first resisted the takeover of these lands by large haciendas. In a nation where 45% of the 90 million population is poor, and where everything he fought for is being reversed, it is hardly surprising that the memory of Zapata has been so easily rekindled. Nor is it surprising that international investors continue to be concerned about instability. According to Mexican economist Jose Luis Calva, some 20 million people are being directly impacted by the dismemberment of the ejidos. Many Indians are being forced off their traditional lands and, facing starvation, are migrating north to seek work on both sides of the border.

Comment: When it all comes down to it, the Rockefeller agenda, similar to Nakusan and Nikko Kaitu, operate to protect what they have. This includes getting back what they lost. Here Rockefeller oil interests, very valuable oil interests, were nationalized by Mexico and Nelson and David have been working since then to get it back. Is NAFTA good for America and Americans? I think the answer is clear. Just as clear as to whom NAFTA best serves. Would Rockefellers impact an entire country to serve their own interests? **Did foreign elitist leaderships in the past take their countries to war to further their own personal interests?**

The point is that while elitist America serves its interests, the concerns of Americans come in a distant second, if really at all. The mask of painting democratic, progressive pictures, to undertake and achieve covert goals is seen via NAFTA and the Rockefellers unending quest to recapture lost assets. *Americans should be so zealous in recapturing their own government.*

David Rockefeller has paid back America for denying his brother Nelson the Presidency; while, he very cleverly runs the country while carrying out Rockefeller agendas to solidify their wealth and power for the foreseeable future. Do the Rockefellers care under what form of government their wealth and power exist? They do, to one degree, that they can control and run it by whatever name it carries, United States of America or Confederation of Nations of Planet Earth. Their form of democracy is where corporate and self-serving agendas dominate, with controlled sprinkling of benefits to those who serve their interests, including crumbs to those who might stand against them.

Does David Rockefeller and all those who have been the beneficiaries of the manipulated economic boom from 1982 through 1996 genuinely care about the plight of other Americans? Yes. Sure. Certainly, to the extent that the failure of all those who live lesser lives can in the future impact, harm, dilute theirs. And if this were not the case, you can bet your bottom dollar that they wouldn't care as reflected as follows by Mr. Rockefeller's own words:

> "....[I]n recent years, business leaders appear to have devoted themselves to making more and more money,

and find themselves with less and less time to devote to civic and social responsibilities and to sinking roots in their communities and showing their loyalty.

The danger, if this current self-serving behavior continues, is that the voice of business will become more muted and the views of business more irrelevant to the important issues of the day. We will find ourselves increasingly marginalized and without the moral authority to demand a hearing from government or the people.

"The profit motive provides the discipline for achievement, but individual goals are formed by the larger society. Our achievements as business leaders only have meaning and value if they embrace and mirror the needs and objectives of the broader society."

Comment: Ironically, openly, David Rockefeller would be the first to probably agree in spirit with the aims of this book in terms of drugs and education. However, your focus and the focus on America should be on getting faithful representation of the American people, not of the American elite. *Their reasons for manifestly speaking against drugs and for improved education are totally different from yours. It also doesn't mean that they want to succeed in what they say.*

There is no purpose to elections if the choice of candidates are beholden to the same core of power, wealth and influence in America. American people don't need attention as an afterthought by the elitist centrix. Many of those within the membership roles believe that these groups serve a legitimate process and program. However, as expressed by the book, their alliance and allegiance to these elitist groups, give the controlling centrix the power and networking to carry on agendas outside the pale of understanding and involvement of its individual members. Thus, it will be necessary for those within these groups to disassociate themselves, and in fact to speak against such a concentration of power and influence by non elected de facto representatives.

The Rockefellers have been the central backers of a number of elitist groups where foreign policy and other matters of government are hashed out by those within its control – usually themselves whether officially or not. This has been of concern to some reflected as follows by the May 5, 1996 excerpt from a Scripps Howard News Service story:

"David Rockefeller clearly isn't used to answering this kind of question.

No, he assures a guest, he does not secretly run the world. For that matter, he doesn't secretly run anything, especially the Trilateral Commission - now entering its 23rd year on the foreign policy map, not to mention the maps of conspiracy theorists. Depending on how you think the world works, the commission is either an international seminar on trade and diplomacy with a revolving membership, or a dank venue of international conspiracy. "Is this an international conspiracy?" he asks as 140 businessmen, academics and government types from Tokyo, New York and Europe parade down the halls of the Waterfront Centre Hotel at the commission's annual meeting.

If so, it is the only conspiracy to post its agenda on the hotel calendar or to assign a press officer to arrange interviews with members for a reporter.

"If I'm running the global conspiracy, I need more staff," said Nick Swales, a bespectacled young Canadian who works for the commission.

These have been tough years for The Trilateral Commission.

Presidential candidates from the right have railed against it. One of its most prominent members, George Bush, fled its roster, fearful he would have to answer to voters demanding to know why he belonged. "It's so absurd I can't help but, to some extent, find it amusing," Rockefeller said. "In another sense, it's put the Trilateral Commission on the map. It's well-known, but little understood."

Apparently.

The map of the world, Trilateral style, stretches from the industrial democracies of Europe, across North America and into Japan. These are the three spots that put the tri- into Trilateral Commission. Its stated intention is to get the Japanese, North Americans and Europeans together to talk about ways to increase international cooperation.

Members range from the well-known - Henry Kissinger, former House speaker Tom Foley - to the obscure. Who has heard of Sirkka Hamalainen? Its members shape opinions. Conrad Black is publisher of the London Telegraph and the Johnstown Tribune-Democrat. **If they go into government service, their membership becomes inactive. Bill Clinton and Warren Christopher can attest to that.**

Showing up at its meetings, conspiracy theorists note, is often followed by rapid advancement in personal achievement: Jimmy Carter joined in 1973 and slept in the White House three years later. Likewise with Bill Clinton. Novelist Mario Vargas Llosa was invited to speak one year and nearly became president of Peru the next.

Not everyone's as certain. Since the mid-1970s, when the commission came to public attention, hard-liners on the political left, and then the far right, latched onto it as a near satanic cabal determined to blanket the globe with a single currency of ambition.

In the early 1970s, David Rockefeller and Zbigniew Brzezinski, then a high-profile professor at Columbia University, attended the annual Bilderberg meeting of international leaders and argued that the meeting ought to let in the Japanese.

Brzezinski became the first director of the commission and, along with Rockefeller and others brought in from Japan and Europe, began assembling a membership list.

Comment: The most important thing to focus on here is that its members stay their membership if they go into "public service." Public service for whom? Plus, if they are misunderstood; from the Trilateral Commission, to the Council on Foreign Relations, to the Council on the Americas etc. etc. why not explain themselves to the American people. Why is it that programs in place from decades before are coming into fruition, including the major one of a single currency, which the U.S. is coercing from the European Union and overriding all objections to it. Does anyone think that one day the U.S. dollar will not be integrated into such a global network?

The point is that major policies and directions of our nation are being directed by outside forces who are controlling everyone inside public service. If you step down from your membership in the council, what does it mean? If you maintain it, does it mean you have to explain it? If so, are they sidestepping the issues? When these elitists groups say they are misunderstood, they may be correct. They wouldn't want anyone to fully understand what they represent and how they operate in diametric opposition to the constitutional mode of government.

The CBS Evening News in a very rare national story, televised on May 2, 1995, reported on David Rockefeller and the Trilateral Commission:

> In recent days we've heard a lot about groups that see the US government as the enemy. But that's not the only enemy they see. Even more suspect is a private group called the Trilateral Commission. It's an exclusive club of business leaders, scholars and politicians. They meet once a year to discuss world problems. But as Anthony Mason reports, some feel the group's agenda is far more sinister.
>
> Mr. CHARLES HECK (The Trilateral Commission): Well, there–there certainly are folks there with–with pretty broad responsibilities, and...
>
> MASON [CBS Reporter]: Charles Heck, North American director, says the Trilateral Commission is hardly secret; you can find it in the phone book, subscribe to its magazines. It was founded to promote global cooperation...
>
> Mr. HECK: ...but this notion of–of what is happening here is a very misguided notion.
>
> Ms. HOLLY SKLAR (Author): The Trilateral Commission is not a conspiracy running the world, but...
>
> MASON: But author Holly Sklar sees the conspiracy theory   gaining momentum.

Ms. SKLAR: I think a lot of people, whether it's in the militia movement or the right in general, are just desperately looking for answers. And unfortunately, oftentimes people latch on to the most simplistic answer they're given.

MASON: They are powerful leaders, but the conspiracy theory that surrounds them may be becoming dangerously influential itself.

Comment: The elitist groups love when right wing groups attack them. They then deploy the forces against right wing groups to diminish their point of view. When Rabin was assassinated, the elitist powers used the psychology of the moment to bend forces against Peres' opposition. They created an environment, through their control of the media and the government, that anyone who supported Netanyahu, anyone who could openly or publicly support anyone but Peres, had to be part of the murder, they were among those who supported Amir's deed in murdering Rabin. This is the very psychology used when any right wing group touches upon a sensitive issue. Are you a right wing thinker? Are you one of them? All this obfuscates the truth. The truth is the elitists number one enemy. Thus, they of course want to be misunderstood or as David Rockefeller himself said "little understood."

The elitist centrix can oppose this book by neglecting it, by attacking its messenger, by litigating against it, or by supporting some to many of its propositions, while at the same time distancing the reader from the book, or misleading the reader that all will be better and things have really started to change.

In the *Seattle Times* story, dated, January 21, 1996, the newspaper pointed to the growing awareness of the American public to problems they simply couldn't put their finger on:

PERU, Ill. - The tumblers of lemonade sit untouched as the talk meanders from the Branch Davidians to plots by the Council on Foreign Relations and the real reasons children no longer learn phonetic reading.

Nine percent answering a Harris Survey thought FBI and ATF actions in Waco, Texas, were taken primarily to kill members of the Branch Davidian sect. One out of 10 answering a Gallup Poll believed the Oklahoma City bombing was a plot out of Washington. The Times Mirror Center for the People and the

Press asked a national sampling of 4,400 people which statement they agreed with:

A) There is simply no excuse for the Oklahoma City bombing.

B) There's no excuse for the bombing, but one can understand the frustrations and anger that may have led people to carry it out.

Fourteen percent of all polled - and 21 percent of regulars on the Internet - chose B.

These few percentage points tucked at the bottom of the surveys represent millions of Americans.

"I was surprised at the response," said Andrew Kohut, director of the Times Mirror Center. "But it supports the impression that there's a larger number of people who have very, very strong views about these kind of things."

Perhaps what disturbs people is the way our leading public representatives admit to love and adherence to the elitist centrix. On May 13, 1996, our Secretary of State, Warren Christopher opened his remarks to the Council of the Americas, as follows:

"Thank you. I am very glad to have the chance to meet with you this morning. I am honored to be back in the distinguished company of Council of the Americas founder David Rockefeller, as well as Chairman John Avery and President Ted Briggs. I especially want to welcome my NAFTA colleagues–Trade Secretary Blanco of Mexico and Trade Minister Eggleton of Canada."

The Vice-President of the United States, Albert Gore, also spoke to the Council of the Americas, saying in part:

"...David Rockefeller and the visionary men and women who joined him to form the Council of the Americas had the wisdom to know that much of the business of America and much of the business of the Americas is business, and that only through dialogue, partnership, and commerce could the shackles of our hemisphere's illiberal past give way to a new era of progress and prosperity.

Today, at long last, I'm happy to say that the new era the Council envisioned is now in full flower. Springtime truly has come to the Americas."

Comment: You can see the very important place our elitist centrix plays in American affairs per the words of the highest public officers in the land. They do not share in the problems of the common American, nor in the problems of the common man in their respective nation. They are unilaterally taking the world onto a course, only they know, and whom they deem are the only ones worthy of knowing, where we are going. They see a global order and power and America is hardly even mentioned in the broad picture of the future "our leaders" paint when outside the camera lens to the American public. Is this loyalty? To whom? Never forget the facade of economic prosperity needed to pursue such an agenda. Thus, a soaring stock market and low interest rates. If Americans had to endure a more realistic economic environment there would be more time and incentive to question what is going on. Thus, since 1982, but for several weeks, we have had an unabated rising stock market, having most Americans forget that what goes up, must come down. During this very time period, as covered by *Recapturing America*, the elitist centrix have assumed control of the world via the powers of the United States of America, its military, it government and its people.

One must remember that the agenda of the centrix elite is to control leadership in dominant, crucial countries - Russia, Israel, Mexico, England, France, Italy, Canada - and otherwise hold on a short least countries such as Japan who have a natural rebellious attitude towards the centrix elite agenda (unless they were in control of it).

One cannot assert that such an agenda is democratic or is Constitutional. The ultimate point is that such an agenda is one that not only taints the election process outside but inside and within, since the U.S. leadership must be aligned with it. Thus corrupt governments have assumed control under the auspices of the centrix elite, who have used the resources of the United States, its people, its government, and its military, to solidify its agenda while masking it by using the Federal Reserve and other U.S. market resources and artificial cooperation to maintain low interest rates, a soaring stock market, and continued consumer spending to keep the economy robust and the populace happy.

All of these actions and this entire agenda are diametrically opposite to the precepts and principles upon which this Nation was founded. So it doesn't matter how persuasive the elitists are in saying they have saved the world from nuclear holocaust and self-destruction, this too, while a satellite benefit of their agenda, is not the reason for their agenda, as Nakusan and Nikko Kaitu would be the first to tell us.

The elitist centrix modus operandi is very simple but effective, as the following two excerpts will attest.

The *Irish Times* in August 1995, immediately after the defeat of Japan in WWIII, noted:

> MR PETER Sutherland has been appointed a member of the international advisory board to the Council on Foreign Relations by the honorary chairman of the council, Mr David Rockefeller. Mr Sutherland is a former Irish EU commissioner and former director-general of the World Trade Organisation.
>
> The newly-established 27-member board includes former heads of state and government, such as Gen Olusegun Obasanjo of Nigeria former ministers and ambassadors a Nobel laureate and human rights leaders, such as Guatemala's Ms Rigoberta Menchu Tum and the Palestinian Dr Hanan Ashrawi Lord Carrington, a former secretary-general of NATO and former British foreign secretary and Baroness Williams, now a professor at Harvard University.

In August 1995, again, post WWIII as described in this book, the *Singapore Straits Times* reported:

> PROFESSOR Chan Heng Chee, head of the Singapore International Foundation and the Institute of Southeast Asian Studies, is among 27 leading world figures appointed to the international advisory board of the prestigious Council on Foreign Relations.
>
> The New York-based council is a research organisation which studies the international aspects of American political, economic and strategic problems. It publishes Foreign Affairs, an influential bi-monthly current affairs journal.
>
> Prof Chan is a former Singapore Permanent Representative to the United Nations. She was named in the latest issue of Asiaweek magazine as one of the region's 21 most powerful women. She has been an international adviser to the Asia-Pacific Foundation of Canada since 1986, and is the former director of the Institute of Policy Studies in Singapore.
>
> Seven other well-known Asians, including former Thai Prime Minister Dr Anand Panyarachun and Mr C. H. Tung, chairman and chief executive officer

of Hongkong's Orient Overseas (International) Ltd, were appointed to the newly-established board.

When Vice-President Gore mentions the shackles of the illiberal past, one hopes that he isn't also saying that new government policies which manipulate facts to distort truth is what he sees as an improvement to the past. During the time of the expansion of the centrix elite agenda, with major corporate downsizing and other major dislocations to the U.S. labor force, many people, from lower level to upper middle level management lost their jobs. If they could not obtain new employment within six months, they weren't counted as unemployed any longer. In this manner, the U.S. painted a prosperous picture by keeping unemployment levels as artificially low as U.S. interest rates.

However, the thrust of this manipulation is that if the entire country became unemployed and did not find work within six months, there would be no unemployment under the government standard! Now, that they have gotten away with these type of machinations and manipulations in accord with the centrix elite agenda, they are using it to manipulate inflation and the CPI and in other ways to further impact those most needing of help and assistance. The worse part of their crime, is that many previously employed people when they looked at the unemployment numbers, figured they were in a very small minority of Americans out of work; frustrated, sad, depressed, suffering humiliation from moving from a hard earned established position, to one where no one wants them at all. If they are to find anything, it is at a fraction of the pay.

These people are a small fraction of the many rowboats yet to sink.

On October 23, 1995, Strobe Talbott, a Rockefeller favorite in the State Department in an address noted:

> In 1954, when David Rockefeller, Otto Wolf, and the other founders of this movable feast gathered for the first time at the Bilderberg Hotel in Oosterbeck, Holland, there was no EU, only a European Coal and Steel Community; the Warsaw Pact did not yet exist; NATO was in only its fifth year of existence, and one of the big issues of the day was whether the alliance should admit the Federal Republic of Germany. But the idea was already there, at Bilderberg, of the West not as a fortress but as an organic, growing community that would, over time, reach out to new members.

The newspaper *The Guardian*, had this to say about the Bilderberg group:

> ".... Bilderberg group, which organises semi-secret, annual three-day meetings of the European-Atlantic great and good from the worlds of business, diplomacy and politics. The first meetings were organised in 1954 by eminence grise Joseph Retinger, the then secretary general of the newly fledged, CIA-funded European Movement. Karl Otto Pohl, then president of Deutsche Bundesbank, David Rockefeller, Lord Carrington and Governor Bill Clinton of Arkansas were among recent delegates. Denis Healey was at that first meeting and, having retired, discusses Bilderberg in his autobiography, The Time Of My Life. Bilderberg is one of the transnational groups suspected by the European-American far Right of being part of the secret elite power structure. Even the Financial Times column `Lombard' has noted: `If the Bilderberg group is not a conspiracy of some sort, it is conducted in such a way as to give a remarkably good imitation of one.' "

The *Toronto Star* in 1996 printed a portion of the guest list:

> "These are some of the participants in the Bilderberg conference.

Lord Carrington

Conference chairman; former NATO secretary-general

Giovanni Agnelli

Honorary chairman, Fiat, Italy

Martti Ahtisaari

President of Finland;

Paul Allaire

Chairman, Xerox, U.S.

Dwayne Andreas

Chairman, Archer-Daniels-Midland, U.S.

Anders Aslund

Carnegie Endowment for International Peace, Sweden

Lloyd Axworthy

Foreign affairs minister, Canada

Francisco Pinto Balsemao

Former prime minister of Portugal

Percy Barnevik

President, ABB Asca Brown Boveri, Sweden

Queen Beatrix

Netherlands

Lloyd Bentsen

Former treasury secretary, U.S.

Franco Bernabe

CEO, Ente Nazionale Idrocarburi, Italy

Carl Bildt

The High Representative

Conrad Black

Chairman, Hollinger, Canada

Frits Bolkestein

Liberal party leader, Netherlands

John Bryan

Chairman, Sara Lee Corp., U.S.

William F. Buckley, Jr.

Editor-at-large, National Review, U.S.

Jaime Carvaja Urquijo

Chairman, Iberfomento, Spain

Jean Chretien

Prime minister of Canada

Bertrand Collomb

Chairman, Lafarge, France

Jon Corzine

Chairman, Goldman Sachs, U.S.

Flavio Cotti

Foreign affairs minister, Switzerland

George David

Chairman, Hellenic Bottling, Greece

Etienne Davignon

Executive chairman, Societe Generale de Belgique,
Belgium

Fredrik Eaton

Chairman, Eaton's, Canada

Gazi Ercel

Governor, Central Bank of Turkey

Stanley Fischer

International Monetary Fund

Al Flood

Chairman, CIBC, Canada

Charles Freeman

Former assistant secretary of defence, U.S.

Emre Gonensay

Foreign affairs minister, Turkey

Allan Gotlieb

Former Canadian ambassador to U.S.

Anthony Griffin

Honorary chairman, Guardian Group, Canada

Mike Harris

Premier of Ontario

Westye Hoegh

Chairman, Leif Hoegh & Co., Norway

Richard Holbrooke

Former assistant secretary of state, U.S.

Jan Huyghebaert

Chairman, Almanij-Kredietbank Group, Belgium

Jaakko Iloniemi

Former Finnish ambassador to U.S.

Peter Job

Chief executive, Reuters Holding, Britain

Lionel Jospin

Socialist party leader, France

Dietrich Karner

Chairman, Erste Allgemeine- Generali
Aktiengesellschaft, Austria

Henry Kissinger

Former U.S. secretary of state

Andrew Knight

News Corp., Britain

Max Kohnstamm

European Policy Centre, Belgium

Henry Kravis

Kohlberg Kravis Roberts, U.S.

Winston Lord

Assistant secretary of state, U.S.

Paul Martin

Finance minister, Canada

Philippe Maystadt

Finance minister, Belgium

Ad P.W. Melkert

Social affairs minister, Netherlands

John Monks

Union leader, Britain

Mario Monti

European commissioner

Sam Nunn

U.S. senator

Andrzej Olechowski

Former foreign affairs minister, Poland

Sylvia Ostry

Centre for International Studies, U of T, Canada

Theodoros Pangalos

Foreign affairs minister, Greece

William Perry

Defence secretary, U.S.

Jan Petersen

Conservative party leader, Norway

David de Pury

Former ambassador, Czech Republic

Malcolm Rifkind

Foreign secretary, Britain

Simon Robertson

Chairman, Kleinwort Benson Group, Britain

David Rockefeller

Chase Manhattan Bank, U.S.

Ted Rogers

President, Rogers Communications, Canada

Renato Ruggiero

Director-general, World Trade Organization

Mona Sahlin

Member of parliament, Sweden

Jurgen Schrempp

Chairman, Daimler-Benz, Germany

Klaus Schwab

President, World Economic Forum

Jack Sheinkman

Chairman, Amalgamated Bank, U.S.

Queen Sofia

Spain

Cornelio Sommaruga

President, Red Cross international committee,
Switzerland

George Soros

President, Soros Fund Management, U.S.

George Stephanopoulos

Senior adviser to the president, U.S.

Gyorgy Suranyi

President, National Bank of Hungary

Peter Sutherland

Former director-general, GATT and WTO, Ireland

Morris Tabaksblat

Chairman, Unilever, Netherlands

J. Martin Taylor

Chief executive, Barclays Bank, Britain

Alex Trotman

Chairman, Ford Motor, U.S.

Antonio Vitorino

Deputy prime minister, Portugal

Franz Vranitzky

Chancellor of Austria

Karel Vuursteen

Chairman, Heineken, Netherlands

John Whitehead

Former deputy secretary of state, U.S.

Red Wilson

Chairman, BCE, Canada

James Wolfensohn

World Bank president

The covert parts of these alliances, as early as 1954, involved the need to control of the media and a control of leaderships throughout the world. These concerns are evident in the following newspaper story from the *Star Tribune*, where writers, Jeff Cohen and Norman Solomon, under a headline, "Elite gathering keeping secrets of public concern," noted on August 28, 1995:

> The founder of USA Today recently gave a speech to 1,500 of this country's most powerful men.

What did he tell them?

Sorry - it's a secret.

Al Neuharth spoke at Bohemian Grove, the all-male encampment in northern California where much of America's government and corporate elite gathers each summer for two weeks of speeches and fun activities like mock-Druid fire rituals.

The Bohemian Grove program identified Neuharth as chairman of the Freedom Forum - a $700-million foundation dedicated to a "free press." So, we might ask: Why did the head of that foundation agree to get together with other power brokers to deliver speeches when everyone present was sworn to secrecy?

The day before his own speech, Neuharth was among 2,200 men who heard an address by House Speaker Newt Gingrich. And what did Gingrich have to say to the assembled movers and shakers? "I'm sorry," Gingrich staff writer Robert George told us. "We do not have a copy of that speech, and it will not be transcribed. The Bohemian Grove events are basically private functions." But matters of great public concern are discussed at Bohemian Grove. The day before Gingrich's speech - with a crucial mass-communications bill gliding through Congress and some humongous media mergers in the offing - a top AT&T executive supplied an assessment of "the complex web of futuristic communications." A week later, former President George Bush spoke at Bohemian Grove. In fact, every Republican president since Coolidge has been a member. Presidential campaigns have been hatched there.

In modern times, participants have included secretaries of state (Henry Kissinger, George Shultz, James Baker), Jimmy Carter, William Randolph Hearst Jr., Walter Cronkite, David Gergen and David Rockefeller. Notables have also included the presidents of such media outlets as CNN and the Associated Press.

All of this gets very little news coverage - a fact that has long frustrated Sonoma County businesswoman Mary Moore, an activist who lives 5 miles from the deluxe camp. "The media trivialize everything about Bohemian Grove," she contends.

Yet, many diligent journalists have tried to report about what goes on there. "The problem is," Moore says, "when the story gets to the top boardrooms, then it gets killed."

Journalist Dirk Mathison found out the hard way.

In July 1991, when Mathison was the San Francisco bureau chief of People magazine (owned by Time Warner), he hiked over back-country trails and sneaked into the Grove's 2,700-acre spread three different times. But on his third foray, Mathison ran into a Time Warner exec who recognized him - and threw him out. Mathison had already learned a lot. For example, a former secretary of the Navy, John Lehman, presented a lecture containing a Pentagon estimate that 200,000 Iraqis were killed during the Gulf War a few months earlier. The Pentagon had not released its death count to the public; at Bohemian Grove, Lehman was more candid.

But Mathison's eyewitness report never made it into the pages of People. The story was mysteriously killed.

The Mathison episode illustrates how difficult it can be for journalists to report fully on America's political and economic elite when their bosses are loyal members of that elite. Today, amid media megamergers and deregulation fervor, the conflict between gathering news and protecting the powerful is more severe than ever."

Comment: The newspaper/print media are in the hands of several families and the national media in the control of the corporate elitist centrix. This alone causes grave concerns, and their role and actions in blocking for the powers behind government, including their absence of journalistic responsibility, clearly evidenced by TWA Flight 800, shows the American people that Americans have to recapture control of their own government. Is it any wonder that the FCC acts with total disdain towards the children of America? Is it any wonder that you have to read *Recapturing America* to understand that the country has to reassert government to its service, not to an elitist centrix, who are the primary beneficiaries of their own self-serving policies and agendas?

Do you as an American know that only a few families exercise central control over the newspapers in this country? Do you know who owns them? Remember Conrad Black, the owner of the *Jerusalem Post, the only Israeli newspaper who supported Netanyahu?* The one who in *Recapturing America* joined Henry Kissinger in a secret meeting with Netanyahu after the latter's surprise victory, to bend Netanyahu to an agenda in diametric opposition to the one he campaigned upon? Look at his credentials as highlighted in the following article from the *Commerce News* (November 1, 1995):

> Mr. Black now controls or influences more than 500 newspapers in Canada, the U.S., the UK, Australia, Israel and the Cayman Islands. The combined circulation of his papers, which include London's Daily Telegraph, exceeds 13 million. His second marriage several years ago in London to journalist Barbara Amiel was front page news; it was attended by his friend Lady Thatcher and celebrities including the Duchess of York. Luminaries including Henry Kissinger, William F. Buckley, Ronald Reagan, Margaret Thatcher are people he counts among his acquaintances.
>
> Black holds a BA from Carleton, an MA from McGill University and a law degree in French from Laval as well as honourary degrees from four universities. A director of the Canadian Imperial Bank of Commerce (CIBC), Brascan, Eaton's of Canada, The Financial Post, Live Entertainment of Canada Inc., Toronto-born Black is a member of several advisory boards including the National Interest, Washington, Gulfstream Aerospace Corp., **Council on Foreign Relations**, New York, Chairman's Council of the Americas Society, **David Rockefeller's Trilateral Commission**, International Institute for Strategic

Studies and he is a patron of the Malcolm Muggeridge Foundation named for the iconoclastic British journalist.

What else is there to say but that you now can read a man's credentials including his organizational affiliations with much more meaning than before. The issues are forged. **This country is headed for a road where we will become a country with the type of elitist government our forefathers fled from. I want my children to live among other children and families who treasure honesty, character and self-sacrifice. The current government trend is to appease the people, to make them as ignorant and desensitized as possible, but as able as possible to accede to the hidden policies and agendas of the centrix elite. This is not a government in accord with our Constitution, the Declaration of Independence and everything else taught in basic civics our government purports to represent. The centrix elite fears YOU, the American people. Stand silent, stand still for too long, and you will be victimized as the country and principles and percepts fought for by those who founded this Nation erode and disappear altogether.** The elitist centrix will move away, overseas, to some new world capital, wherever they decide, and America will be no more or no less at first than any part of the new world federation or whatever they will call it. However, the American citizen will have been trampled upon and eviscerated by a government which in no way serves him or her or their children, and those who have all the power and wealth in essence **will have used this country to solidify their own gains and interests**.

The *centrix elite consist of unelected powers* being the puppet masters over puppets offered to us to choose among; any one, or combination of which, once chosen into office, becomes in essence under the full control of those who pull his or her strings albeit giving up their elitist group membership or participation. With this type of control, you obtain full control of the media and all other facets of government and communication, which results in allowing the desensitization of Americans and their children, their victimization and the open insult of coyly denying Americans the truth of Oklahoma City and TWA Flight 800.

The way the FBI is being directed to handle TWA Flight 800 **compels complicity under the name of "national security," or "national interests," by otherwise loyal FBI agents.** This type of excuse for obfuscation, lies, and deceptions, is only warranted under a state of war or declared emergency by the U.S. Congress.

You must ask politicians to self-sacrifice and make commitments which they must honor or they must step down and out of office. This saves the need for extremists shouting to put politicians to lie detector tests to see if they are aligned with certain groups or not. This would put the country on another polarized road, one with its own problems, and one which the centrix elite says that it has freed the world from. Thus, while there is a need to know where politicians do stand, *obtain it from commitments to succeed in limited time frames.* Further, while this permits some of the centrix elite to hide behind it, I believe that many in these groups can't see the forest from the trees. They only see the power, the wealth, the networking, and their own self-interests. There may be many good people among them moving in the wrong direction. The purpose of *Recapturing America* is to help bring clarity to what is going on and to catalyze forces and energies to move in the right direction to protect and save our nation. If the American people want to move for a global order, then let it be their choice. But if they are not told, nor asked, then those who operate such an agenda are on seriously flawed grounds and subject to serious reproach.

May those who have been coerced into false directions, stand up to assure that government remains in control of the people, my beloved fellow citizens of the United States of America, who cherish honesty, character and self-sacrifice, and who want a leadership and media who directs their energies towards such correct and noble goals.

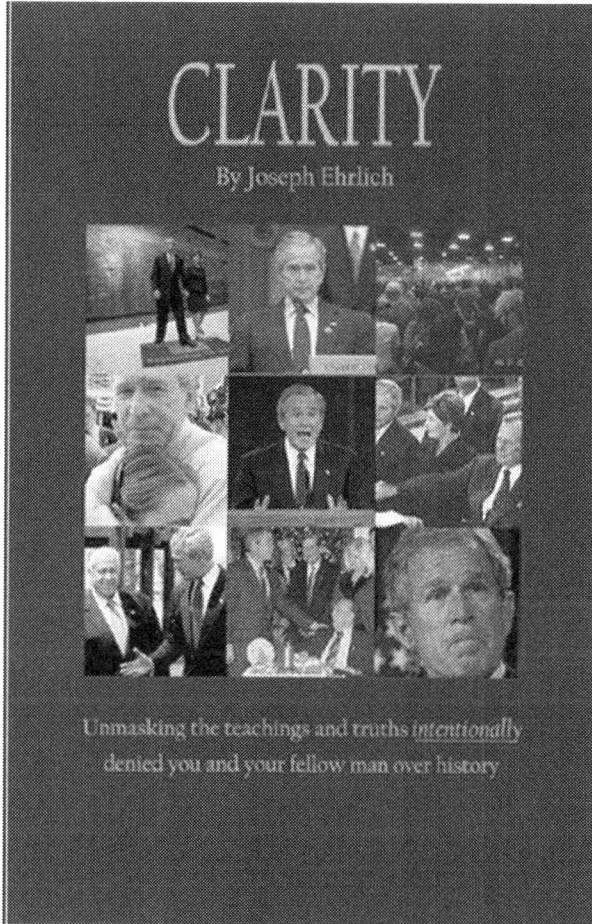

CLARITY
By Joseph Ehrlich

Unmasking the teachings and truths *intentionally* denied you and your fellow man over history

ISBN: 978-0-6151-4142-8

www.ingramcontent.com/pod-product-compliance
Lightning Source LLC
Chambersburg PA
CBHW052009090426

42741CB00008B/1610